GOLF
ASTROLOGY

Also available from Random House Value Publishing:

Golf Ching

The Golf Omnibus

The Illustrated History of Golf

The Ultimate Golf Trivia Book

GOLF
ASTROLOGY

Michael Zullo

GRAMERCY BOOKS
NEW YORK

This 2001 edition is published by Gramercy Books™,
an imprint of Random House Value Publishing, Inc.,
280 Park Avenue, New York, New York 10017,
by arrangement with Andrews McMeel Publishing.

Gramercy Books™ and design are trademarks of Random House Value Publishing, Inc.

Random House
New York · Toronto · London · Sydney · Auckland
http://www.randomhouse.com/

Printed and bound in the United States of America

Library of Congress Cataloging-in-Publication Data
Zullo, Michael.
　　Golf astrology / Michael Zullo.
　　　　p. cm.
　　Originally published: Kansas City, MO : Andrews McMeel Pub., 2000.
　　ISBN 0-517-16353-5
　　1. Astrology. 2. Golf—Miscellanea. I. Title.
　　BF1729.G64 Z85 2001
　　133.5'8796352—dc21　　　　　　　　　　　　　00-066314

8 7 6 5 4 3 2 1

To Judy Droder, who has battled her way
out of the sand traps and bunkers of life
to reach the top of the leaderboard in courage
and determination.

Contents

Preface

Let me state for the record that my love for golf far exceeds my ability to play it. As much as I enjoy the game, astrology is my true passion—a subject that I have studied for more than thirty years.

After spending sixteen years as an executive for IBM, I followed the stars to Key West, Florida, and opened a new-age store. Combining my professional expertise and my knowledge of astrology, I created a commercial computer program to chart personalized astrological profiles.

In my ongoing studies of this remarkable science, I began examining the relationship between the twelve sun signs of the zodiac and different pastimes such as fishing, gardening, and golfing. It was quite revealing. The heavens really do have a strong influence on our leisure activities.

After I'd charted my horoscope and those of my golfing buddies, the insights we learned from our charts helped us understand more about our natural traits and tendencies. By applying this knowledge to our golf games, we actually managed to lower our handicaps and get more enjoyment out of our rounds together.

For example, I'm a Cancer. One of the many things I discovered through astrology is that the key to a successful game for my sign is to play methodically. I shouldn't let anyone force me to play faster or slower than I want to. My body has a unique rhythm, and if I orient my pace to that rhythm, I tend to shoot well.

In this book I have collected my findings about the link between golf and astrology in hopes of helping readers better understand themselves and become the golfers they were born to be.

Fore!thoughts

The zodiac may tell you more about your golf game than any scorecard can. And that's no bogey.

You see, astrology is a science based on the melding of astronomy, mathematics, and psychology. The positions of the planets, moon, and sun at the moment of your birth will influence the way you behave at home, in the office—and on the golf course. Depending on where and when you were born, the energy fields from the alignment of the planets, moon, and sun help shape all the traits that make you unique.

You were born under one of the twelve sun signs (for example, Aries is from March 21 to April 20). Each sign has certain positive and negative characteristics. Astrologically, the sun is the most powerful of the celestial forces, having a dominant influence on personality and behavior. The traits described in this book are based on sun-sign astrology, which is quite accurate—but it isn't flawless without more detailed astrological charts. Like fingerprints, every person has his or her unique chart. However, people born under the same sign tend to have the same general tendencies, whether they display them openly or not.

Can astrology really help you on the golf course? Have you ever rimmed out a two-footer? Shanked a drive in the woods? Plunked a sleeve of balls in the drink? Of course astrology can help you.

Golf Astrology is designed to give you a celestial boost on the fairway. As golf becomes increasingly high-tech, this book will try to balance your game through the no-tech approach of astrology. It can help you discover your innate strengths, weaknesses, and instincts so you can become a better golfer and get added pleasure out of the game. The more you learn about your natural tendencies, the easier it is to apply them in your daily life—and on the golf course.

You might be golfing a certain way that goes contrary to your astrological traits. This book will help you get in touch with who you really are as a golfer. Once you realize this, you then can make the appropriate adjustments. By playing golf with an understanding of your true self, you will enjoy the game more and lower your score.

Let's say, for example, you're an Aries. Because of your astrological tendencies, you're probably impatient, aggressive, and temperamental on the course. Once you've recognized these characteristics, you might focus on playing under control at all times and golfing with a steady rhythm and tempo.

You can read this book to learn about the golfing traits of all your playing partners too. You'll get a clearer awareness of how they play the game and how they relate to you and to various situations on the course.

Remember, not everyone who shares the same sign is going to act or golf exactly alike. This is certainly true of professional golfers. Even though some of the pros were born under your sign, they obviously play a game far different from yours. They may have many of your sign's traits, but the pros are affected by other astrological influences that have dominated their lives.

Golf Astrology gives the astrological signs of the top golfers on the PGA, LPGA, and Senior Tour and uses examples of their past performances as well as quotes to illustrate various sun-sign traits. This way, you can identify the similarities in personality, style of play, and other characteristics among the pros who belong to your sign.

For example, Taurus players such as John Daly have a tendency to be bullheaded. At the 1998 Bay Hill Invitational, Daly sank five straight balls into the drink with his three-wood because he refused to alter his shot or change his club. "I had the courage to do it [try to carry the water], but I just didn't have the wisdom to bail out," he ruefully admitted later.

If nothing else, finding out which pros are born under your sign allows you to connect with the game's top players. The more you relate to the astrological instincts, traits, and powers of the pros who share your birth sign, the better player you can become.

No sign has exclusive rights to any specific golfing characteristic because humans and the game itself are so complex. However, we are all intertwined in the zodiac by one of the four astrological elements—fire, earth, air, or water.

Aries, Leo, and Sagittarius are fire signs. These golfers display enthusiastic, dynamic personalities. On the course, they tend to play fast, take risks, and bet big.

Taurus, Virgo, and Capricorn are earth signs. These golfers are usually very grounded people who usually take a slower, more disciplined approach to the game.

Gemini, Libra, and Aquarius are air signs. Although these golfers can sometimes play inconsistently, they are extremely inventive and adaptable on the course.

Cancer, Scorpio, and Pisces are water signs and the most sensitive golfers of the zodiac. They often display incredible intuition in their shot-making decisions.

In a classic example of how astrological influences affect professional golf, fire-sign golfers have won the fewest times at the British Open of any golfers from all four astrological elements. Because of their energy, daring, and temperament, fire-sign golfers seem to burn out too quickly. Air-sign golfers—which include Aquarians Jack Nicklaus, Greg Norman, and Nick Price—have won the most British Open titles. That's because Aquarians are so inventive and seem to adapt better than most to the unpredictable weather and erratic playing conditions that characterize the British Open.

What are your natural-born golfing assets? *Golf Astrology* can help you discover them. Each of the book's twelve chapters—one for each sun sign—is divided into several sections. They are:

★ A profile of the sign, explaining general tendencies and personalities and how they relate to golf.

★ An explanation of how to choose the kind of golf equipment best suited to your astrological sign.

★ A description of the clothes and colors you should wear on the golf course based on your sign.

★ An explanation of how best to prepare physically and mentally for a round of golf for your particular sign.

★ Suggestions on how to use your astrological tendencies to improve your drives, short game, hazard play, putting, and course management.

★ An explanation of how to bet on the course by following your sign.

★ A description of the kinds of conversations you're best suited to engage in while playing.

★ Suggestions on the best and worst times for you to tee off based on your sign.

★ A rating that compares your compatibility with that of your playing partners based on their signs. A birdie means that, for you, it's an excellent pairing astrologically; a bogey means it's fair or poor; a par means it's a good pairing under most circumstances.

How you interact with your fellow golfers and how they respond to you are both critical to your enjoyment of this wonderful sport. If you're getting along, chances are you're astrologically harmonious. If you aren't, it doesn't mean you should never be in the same foursome again. It simply implies that you both possess strong tendencies that appear incompatible. However, there are many other factors that can overcome these differences. In any case, try to understand—and even appreciate the contrasts—and make any adjustments necessary for a better golfing relationship.

So go ahead and have fun with *Golf Astrology*—and with the game we all love. Let the cosmos caddie you to longer drives and shorter putts, more birdies and fewer bogeys, heightened enjoyment and lower handicaps.

Seve Ballesteros

Mark Brooks

Jim Gallagher Jr.

Davis Love III

Joey Sindelar

Dana Quigley

Helen Alfredsson

Donna Andrews

Pat Bradley

JoAnne Carner

Meg Mallon

the**aries**golfer

energetic

demonstrative

very competitive

fast-playing

aggressive

(March 21 – April 20)

Aries is the first sign of the zodiac, making you one of the most dynamic signs in the astrological cycle.

As an Aries, you tend to be an active, high-spirited, demonstrative person. When it comes to golf, you like to play it your way, not necessarily by the book. You tend to make it up as you go along.

Your sign is the most competitive in the zodiac, which means you want your playing partners to be competitive as well. You golf best when you're playing with others who are self-confident and move the game along quickly.

Golf can be a bittersweet painting to you. At times, your swing is as fluid as an artist's brush stroke, and all is right with the world. At other times, your swing seems as out of place as an errant splat of black paint.

Seve Ballesteros could be the poster boy for Aries. He can charm the hide off a rattlesnake—but he also can act like one too. Seve's touch around the greens is that of the consummate master, yet his wayward drives, long irons, and approach work are that of a tortured genius.

Like Seve, you attack the course from every angle, often from the rough, and are determined to knock down flag-sticks. But as intense as you are, you can be very self-effacing too.

▼

During the first round of the 1998 British Open, Seve Ballesteros, as usual, was missing the fairways with regularity. At one point he told his playing partners, "I am spending so much time in the rough, these people [spectators] think I am the steward."

After whacking two drives into an adjoining parking lot, JoAnne Carner teed up another ball, turned to the gallery, and said, "Well, that lot's full. Let's see if I can park this baby someplace else."

▲

Because of your high energy, you get easily frustrated when you're behind a foursome of dawdlers and duffers. You hate to have anything louse up the rhythm and flow of your game. However, you're generous with advice to others on how to play a certain shot. Because of this and your spirited golf, it's not hard for you to find willing partners who enjoy playing with you. If you can control that Aries temper whenever things don't go your way, you have the potential to be one of the best golfers on the course.

If a few lip-outs or banana balls don't ignite your temper, they could very easily jangle your nerves, so it's important to find a way to keep cool. But don't listen to others. Stick with a calming technique that works for you.

Helen Alfredsson let tournament pressure and her nervous personality trigger one of the greatest collapses in a major in LPGA history. In the 1994 U.S. Women's Open, she had set the eighteen-hole Open scoring record with a 63 in the opening round and had a seven-stroke lead after forty-three holes. But over the next eighteen holes, Helen went 14-over. She staggered over the final eleven holes and eventually finished tied for ninth.

"I tried to do the calm thing, do what everybody says you're supposed to do," she told reporters later. "But it didn't work. I think you have to work with what you have, and not against what you are."

▲

The key for you is to play with rhythm, tempo, and balance. Don't make any drastic changes in your swing or swing thoughts.

Equipment

You want the very best in equipment, especially customized clubs, because you tend to be somewhat status conscious. You believe they will not only give you an edge on the course but also impress your playing partners.

However, you're a realist too, and custom clubs may be too expensive for you. Nevertheless, buy the best set you can afford until you reach that level in your game where you can rationalize the cost of custom clubs.

While it's important to try many different clubs, you probably won't waste a lot of time doing this—even though you should—because you're so eager to play golf.

As for putters, forget about all those specs like: Is it polar balanced? Is the carbon steel milled? Does it have a short neck? Take the time to try different putters until you find one that simply feels right for you, regardless of all the hype or expense.

Attire

The Greek god of war was named Aries, a.k.a. Mars in Roman times. Today we know Mars as the red planet, so the typical Aries loves red. Red anything. It's a strong color that represents energy, strength and aggressiveness, and should be the dominant color in your golfwear. Stay away from cool colors because they go against the very nature of your competitiveness.

As for the rest of your outfit, you're a classic sort of person and usually one of the best-dressed golfers on the course. And why not? You like to be noticed.

Game Preparation

When you arrive at the course, which in your case should be at least an hour before tee time, you need to practice, practice, practice. This is something you don't like to do, because you get bored easily—and practice to you is boring. But think about your desire to win. That one hour of practice can make all the difference in the world.

You also should limber up with stretching and shoulder exercises more than other golfers since you need to release your pent-up energy. This energy is quite often responsible for staccato or jerky motions in your swing.

Remember, Aries, concentration is not one of your strong traits. Practice will help make things more routine so you won't get bogged down in thinking of the mechanics of your swing.

However, your swing can betray you from time to time. In your pregame practice, don't worry if suddenly you're hitting a different kind of shot. Golf with whatever shot you have on that particular day. Don't get uptight about it.

▼

Before the final round of the 1998 Longs Drugs Challenge, Donna Andrews went to the practice range and discovered that she was hitting a cut rather than her usual draw. Instead of panicking or fiddling with her swing, Donna accepted the fact she had to play with a different shot and wound up winning the tournament.

▲

Your Game

Off the Tee

You're strong and full of energy. You tend to attack the ball with more power than thoughtful follow-through. It's important to pay attention to stance, grip, alignment, and weight shift on your drives. If your concentration is faltering, you tend to smack a fat shot. Errant drives are also due to your impatience and your tendency to swing too fast. So slow down, especially on the backswing. Worse than the embarrassment of a bad shot is the severe dent it could put in your ego.

On the Fairway

You're the proverbial risk taker, and this is especially true with your irons. You're not afraid to use a nine-iron when a seven would do for most. This is again because of your strength and energy. But there's another factor—your intuitive powers. You almost instinctively know which is the right club for you when faced with a difficult shot. Don't bother taking the advice from others. Trust your instincts here. You're usually right. That doesn't mean that every shot is perfect, but it does mean that it probably was the right club to use in that situation.

In the Hazard

This is the most difficult part of your game because you must battle more than just your predicament. You have to battle your anger, your ego, and—if things really get bad— your nerves.

But you've been in this situation many times before, so you shouldn't let a bad lie cause you too much grief. Just keep your rage in check, because otherwise it'll only get worse. Take those deep breaths now and picture that ball landing pin-high on the green.

If your ball is paying regular visits to the bunkers, you face another potential problem: your tendency to let the hazards stifle the great enthusiasm you showed at the first tee. You'll lose interest in the game and just want to get the round over with. Do what Ballesteros does. Make each hazard a challenge. Attack the ball—but without anger. Your chances of getting up and down will be greatly enhanced.

On the Green

If there's ever a moment for you to slow down, it's here on the green. You need to take the time to figure out all the elements of the green: speed, type of grass, wetness, and pitch. It's natural for you to be aggressive, but make sure you have all the facts before stroking the ball. Also, use your visualization skills too.

▼

Poor putting cost Davis Love III at the 1995 U.S. Open, where he tied for fourth place. His shocking three-putt on the 72nd hole at the 1996 U.S. Open knocked him out of a possible spot in a play-off. But he won the 1997 PGA Championship by making several tough putts. "If you're thinking you're going to make them, and you're being patient, you can make some of them," he said.

▲

Course Management

You have a tendency to play golf using the same strategy as a steely-eyed army general—a merciless scorched-earth policy. You take no prisoners. And you shoot from every which way—out of the bunker, beside a tree, behind the green. You're not afraid to attempt the risky shot, but it's wise to curb some of your aggressive nature in certain situations. The tough part is learning when to play it smart and when to take a chance.

You're quite creative in your shots and you don't waste a lot of time. But you should try to slow down, if for no other reason than to give your imagination the time to figure out the best shot.

The bottom line: You have to play the game your way or you won't play it at all.

▼

After winning the 1997 PGA Championship, his first major, Davis Love III said, "I didn't try too hard. I tried to enjoy it. I tried to have fun. I tried to let my game come out."

▲

Don't let that Aires temper take control of you if you make a bad shot. You need to demonstrate that just because you threw your wedge in the water the last time, it won't happen again. Count to ten or take a deep breath and allow the rage to pass. It's guaranteed to save you a few strokes.

Wagering

Betting definitely adds to the fun of golf, especially for you. Always the risk taker and gambler, you can't wait to wager on the game. Shooting well is one thing; but winning the pot is even sweeter to you. You favor automatic presses, so the stakes rise, which makes you a better golfer (assuming you keep your anger and nerves under control).

You have a tendency to get cocky when you're winning. Be careful about mouthing off to your opponents, because your words could come back to haunt you. And don't offer advice on how to play to any partner who's losing, even if it is in your nature to be helpful. Most of all, be careful about getting too smug with your presses. Early on the back nine, just when you're thinking that you've cleaned out your opponent, you could end up with empty pockets.

▼

Meg Mallon, who had nine top-ten finishes in the first eight months of 1998 but no victories, said she could have won "probably one hundred percent of them." But her mind kept wandering during the final round. "I'd be making my victory speech on the ninth hole," she said. "They say play one shot at a time, but it's hard to do because there's so much time to think between shots."

▲

Let's Talk

Don't talk business, at least for a while, during the game. If you go to the course with the intention of closing a deal or telling the boss your latest and greatest accomplishment, you probably won't achieve either goal. You're a fast-acting person who likes to get to the point. But make golf the point and have fun out there. If your playing partner wants to talk about business or a serious topic, try to keep it casual. You have a tendency to get too intense, which can throw your game out of kilter.

Wait for the 19th hole, and even then first talk about the game. But be careful not to poke too much fun at your playing partners for the way they played. And don't whine if you played poorly. You could end up in an embarrassing situation, especially since your big voice can be heard throughout the clubhouse.

Tee Time

You're not really a morning person, so the best tee times for you are later in the day. In fact, during the summer, try to get off work early so you can get out on the course in midafternoon.

Because you're a fire sign, you play well in the heat. In fact, the hotter the better. You seem to gain strength as the game goes on, while your playing partners wilt.

Playing Partners

Birdies

GEMINI: This golfer is a challenge for you, and that can be fun. You especially like the verbal jousting and mind games that Gemini initiates.

LEO: You both like to play fast, high-energy golf and thrive on each other's enthusiasm. Everyone on the course knows when you two are playing. The conversation is never boring.

SAGITTARIUS: You both play fast and hard, leaving the rest in the rough. Sag's spirited energy matches yours, making for a fun, active time on the course.

AQUARIUS: You're both strong individuals who find each other stimulating on and off the links. While not a big gambler, Aquarius's personable nature helps make this a good pairing.

Bogeys

TAURUS: If you enjoy wagering on the course, forget about playing with Taurus, because this golfer is no risk taker. Taurus loves to stick to routines that can be downright annoying to you.

CANCER: Emotionally, you don't understand each other and don't play golf the same way. Watch what you say to this supersensitive golfer or else your blunt comments could put a damper on the game.

SCORPIO: You can identify with Scorpio's competitive nature, but eventually this golfer will say or do something that ignites your temper or disrupts your rhythm.

PISCES: With Pisces, the game for you becomes excruciatingly annoying, driving you to distraction. Especially vexing is this golfer's gamesmanship.

Pars

ARIES: Playing with someone like you could be fun for a while, but be wary of two large egos. They might clash somewhere over the last four or five holes.

VIRGO: While you don't like to take advice, you could learn a lot from Virgo's analytical mind. But Virgo has a tendency to be slow and get on your nerves.

LIBRA: You can have an enjoyable round together, as long as you both share the same cultural background. However, Libra can slow your game down.

CAPRICORN: You both play the game with intensity and enjoy the competition. But be careful, because you both know how to trigger each other's volatile temper.

Stewart Cink

John Daly

Jim Furyk

Hal Sutton

Bob Tway

Lee Westwood

Jim Dent

John Mahaffey

Johnny Miller

Dale Eggeling

Liselotte Neumann

Wendy Ward

Betsy Rawls

the**taurus**golfer

practical

easygoing

dependable

consistent

stubborn

(April 21 – May 21)

You're the most practical in all the zodiac, and concern for the necessities of life is paramount in your life.

John Daly and Johnny Miller represent the two extremes of the Taurus: Daly is the undisciplined, grip-it-and-rip-it terror on the course; Miller, the consummate, deliberate fair-haired linksman.

You're a very grounded person and have an uncomplicated nature. You're not as competitive as most. A friendly game of golf with the same partners each Saturday gives you the comfort level that you require in order to enjoy this sport.

Even when your ball doesn't go where you intended, it won't upset you that much. Golf is still just a game to you. Being with your friends and having a good time is more important than breaking 80. In fact, sometimes you're surprised when you beat everyone else.

▼

When the LPGA's Dale Eggeling won the 1998 Los Angeles Women's Championship, she admitted, "I never even thought about winning. I didn't think I had a chance."

▲

You like to take your time, keep the conversation going, and not be pressured into moving along too fast just because someone behind you is in a hurry. You're most likely to let others play through. You enjoy playing the same course, and because you're so dependable and organized, you're probably involved in setting up tournaments or are an officer of the country club.

You have a good handle on who you are as a person and as a player. You have confidence in your game, but that confidence tends to waver when you absolutely, positively have to make that putt or nail that approach.

In the two years previous to winning the 1998 Las Vegas Invitational, Jim Furyk had finished in the top ten in twenty-three tournaments without a victory.

"I've always had confidence in myself that I'm good enough to win a golf tournament," said Furyk. "There was no doubt. But every time you come close, it seems that much harder to get over the hill. I've been saying for two years I'm not putting any pressure on myself, but, yeah, it starts to bother you."

As your symbol of the bull shows, you're stubborn. Once you make up your mind on how to play a shot, you won't change. Even when your club selection or mechanics prove you were wrong, you continue to do the same thing when faced with an identical situation again. As a result, an otherwise good round can be ruined by ghastly scores on one or two holes.

▼

In 1998, John Daly, had several horrific holes—a nine at the Masters, two nines at the MCI Classic, a ten at the British Open, and a ten at the Las Vegas Invitational. But his biggest number of the year was the eighteen he took on the fifth hole in the final round of the Bay Hill Invitational, where he hit his first six shots—including five straight three-woods—into the lake. "It wasn't that I didn't care," he insisted. "I just lost my patience. I had the courage to do it [carry the lake], but I just didn't have the wisdom to bail out."

▲

Equipment

You're not only a creature of habit but a creature of comfort. You aren't likely to need or want the latest technological marvels in club design. For you, the clubs need to feel right. The clubs you choose should be on the more conventional side. Stay away from radically shaped clubs. If you're a typical Taurus, you're strong but you tend to be stocky, always fighting the battle of the bulge. Because you tend to swing slower than most golfers, you might want to consider very flexible shafts to get extra distance.

Once you buy your clubs, you probably will play with

the same set until the day they cart you off the course. You tend to get attached to things. You may even use the same old putter your father used, not because it's old, but because it was your father's.

▼

When Johnny Miller made his Senior Tour debut in 1997, he used an old putter—an ugly, jerry-built contraption that was eight inches longer than normal and swollen with adhesive tape.

▲

Attire

Comfort is the most important element in your clothes. You should look for loose-fitting cotton garments, and keep the colors conservative. You'd prefer not to stand out, unlike the neon golfer in yellow pants and an aqua shirt. The colors that serve you best on the course are blues and greens.

Your golf shoes should be dark and have an understated quality about them.

Game Preparation

Since you don't like to hurry, make sure you arrive early at the course. While splitting time between the driving range and the putting green, find the time to socialize with other club members. It's all part of your game preparation—because you want to feel that everything is in its right place and that the other players are as comfortable as you are.

If you don't already, you should have a pregame routine. This should include some warm-up exercises, which you don't especially like but know are necessary. If you're a typical Taurus, your body isn't limber, so you need to do stretching movements to help you avoid pulling a muscle. But you tend to make your warm-up nothing more than carrying your clubs from your car to the cart and swinging the club a few times.

To satisfy your practical side, you need to make sure that everything is ready: new golf balls, plenty of tees, water bottle, and a few candy bars (chocolate, of course). You usually are the first one at the course to greet the others in your foursome. They expect that, because you've been doing it that way for years.

Despite some misgivings on your part, consider getting some lessons from a pro, if only to sharpen your mechanics.

▼

Hal Sutton, who won the 1983 PGA Championship, suggests that you spend time trying to find the right professional. "Get with somebody who knows your game and stay with that person. Each and every one of us has a unique fingerprint. When you start trying to change that fingerprint, that's when things go wrong. The same is true with golf."

▲

Your Game

Off the Tee

The greatest asset of your game is your predictability. You hit the ball off the tee the same way virtually every time you play. You can concentrate easily because of the familiarity of your tee shot. Your swing may be slow, but your power is strong. The biggest variable to you is the speed and direction of the wind. Once you take this into account, you usually hit a solid shot far down the fairway. In fact, you probably hit your drives farther than any of your playing partners.

On the Fairway

Take your time to analyze the situation. Check your grip and stance, and then take a few practice strokes. For you, the best approach shots are those short chips around the green.

If you find that your short game isn't going well, it's only because you strayed from the basics. You're usually a consistent golfer who has calibrated each club and knows its distance exactly. You also tend to feel quite comfortable with the course because you've been playing it for years. However, if you're on a new course, you need to take more time before each shot to assess the situation.

In the Hazard

Rarely do you land in a hazard, but if you do, don't look for some novel way to extricate yourself. Avoid risky shots, even if advice to the contrary comes from one of the best players in your foursome.

Your biggest problem is your determination to hit the same shot with the same club again and again. If at first you don't succeed, try a different strategy.

On the Green

You love using that old putter; it's as comfortable as that old easy chair in your family room. You've wielded it for years and know exactly what it can do for you. Putting is a strong part of your game, although you should watch out for your tendency to stroke the ball a little too lightly. Your conservative nature, which promotes a fear of rolling the ball past the cup, has always been a bugaboo for you.

If something bad happens on the green, it's vital to keep your composure.

▼

On his way to winning his first PGA event, the 1998 Freeport-McDermott Classic, Englishman Lee Westwood had his mettle tested on the 14th hole. Attempting a thirty-footer from the fringe, Westwood, who was holding on to a slim lead, saw his ball pop up and strike the top of his putter blade on the follow-through, for a one-stroke penalty. He still faced a ten-foot putt for bogey. But he didn't even flinch and rammed the ball into the cup. "You have to hole the putts when they count," he said.

▲

Course Management

You have good analytic skills, so use them in your course management. Know your limitations and pick the safer route to the hole. You don't need to take a lot of risks. For example, while others may try to reach the green with a long iron, you should look to lay up. You don't want to find your ball in a bunker or in the drink.

Because you know the kind of distance you get from each club, you generally use good judgment in club selection. Although this trait suits you well, you have a tendency to stick with the same shot and club selection even when you've made a poor decision. You need to take into consideration everything from how you feel physically that day to the weather conditions and make the necessary adaptations. But that is sometimes hard for you.

You have your swing down pat, but that doesn't mean you shouldn't concentrate. Be careful about letting your mind wander.

▼

Says Hal Sutton: "You get a little complacent when you're not paying attention to what you should be doing, and then you do things that cause you to lose your confidence. All of a sudden, you start searching. Yeah, it can happen to anybody.

"I never take golf for granted. I did that once. Just when you think it's easy and you've got the world by the tail, it jumps up and bites you."

▲

Usually if you go against your natural conservative, play-it-safe tendencies, you end up in trouble.

▼

At the 1998 Buick Open, Jim Furyk was locked in a play-off with J. P. Hayes. On the first play-off hole, Furyk faced a three-wood shot from light rough. Although he had a bad lie, he went against his Taurean nature to lay up and make par. "I thought it was time to be aggressive," he recalled. "It was probably the wrong shot. I hit it very solidly but the rough caught it." Moments later, Furyk lost the play-off.

▲

Wagering

You're not big on wagering, but for the sake of the others, you partake in a friendly bet. However, you feel that you shouldn't put your hard-earned money in jeopardy. Be sure you understand the betting game and keep the wagers small. You need to make it simple or frustration will set in, and that not only makes you angry but ultimately costs you cash.

You're not good at playing mind games with your golf partners because you're a straightforward person. Watch out for presses, since they could create stress for you. You must rely on your physical game to win.

What you shouldn't tolerate is gamesmanship—someone rattling coins in his or her pocket or coughing just as you're about to putt. If you feel a fellow golfer is deliberately trying to psych you out, you can truly become a raging bull. Vent if you must. Your words won't be forgotten and will definitely startle your partners. You know you have this temper, although hopefully you know how to keep it in check. But there are times when you need to speak out. After all, gamesmanship goes against your very nature.

Let's Talk

Don't bother bringing up serious issues or business talk on the golf course. If, on the other hand, a playing partner does, you should naturally join in the conversation. You prefer having business discussed in the office or at other settings away from the course. The same is true when talking about serious subjects. The reason is simple: Golf is a game to enjoy; it's an escape from the real world.

Besides, you're tough and savvy when it comes to business. In fact, you can be ruthless. But that's in the business world, not on the fairways. Also, you don't want any surprises in a business conversation, because you like to be prepared and have all the facts. You can't always do that on the course.

Preserving your enjoyment and comfort on the links should be absolutely paramount to your golf game.

Tee Time

You're not an early-morning person, so pick a tee time later in the morning or in the afternoon if possible.

Weather affects your ability to play. You're an earth sign who likes the coolness of spring and fall. The high heat of summer is difficult for you, and you tend to perspire heavily. During the summer months, try to set an early tee time—but not too early.

You also like playing on the weekends more than week-days. You're very organized and find that you can easily separate work from play in this way.

Playing Partners

Birdies

CANCER: You're both conservative and reliable, and you have similar goals. When your game is down, Cancer encourages and inspires you and gets you to extend yourself.

VIRGO: The two of you are in tune with each other. You both play the game with a solid commitment, although very slowly and deliberately with little pressure.

CAPRICORN: You make a good pair because you both play disciplined, consistent golf. Capricorn's hard work and dedication can inspire you to play better.

PISCES: Neither of you takes golf all that seriously, but you both like the routine of a weekly game. This golfer's easygoing manner appeals to you.

Bogeys

ARIES: With Aries' quick temper and high-stakes gambling, you may find yourself in an uncomfortable situation. Besides, this golfer will prod you to hurry.

SCORPIO: You can get annoyed by Scorpio's mysterious nature. Also, Scorpio's intensity and competitiveness tend to clash with your easygoing nature.

SAGITTARIUS: You two aren't very compatible on the golf course. Sag wants to play fast and impulsively, while you want to play slow and deliberately.

AQUARIUS: This golfer's eccentric ways and inconsistent golf can drive you nuts. You're also likely to find Aquarius's swagger too much to handle.

Pars

TAURUS: You understand each other on and off the course. This match-up is enjoyable until there's a disagreement—then neither one of you will budge.

GEMINI: You might find Gemini charming and fun on the golf course. But this golfer's wild betting and unpredictable nature can try your patience.

LEO: You're fairly compatible, although you both have strong personalities that can at times clash. When Leo wants to bet big, you won't be happy.

LIBRA: You generally enjoy playing with Libra, but this golfer can be a little too witty for your tastes. Libra's needling can sometimes irk you.

Olin Browne

Mark Calcavecchia

Fred Funk

John Huston

Hale Irwin

Justin Leonard

Andrew Magee

Phil Mickelson

Steve Pate

Craig Stadler

Jim Albus

Brian Barnes

David Graham

Sam Snead

Janice Moodie

Tina Barrett

Sandra Haynie

the**gemini**golfer

unpredictable

talkative

adaptable

inconsistent

fast-playing

(May 22 – June 21)

No one can ever accuse you of being boring or predictable. Represented in the zodiac by the dual sign of the twins, you have two personalities that are not at all similar. Your golf is like that too, because you can be playing like Sam Snead on the front nine and Sam Spade on the back nine. You just never know which personality will show up on the course.

▼

At the 1998 British Open, defending champion Justin Leonard shot 73-73 before misfiring in the third round with a horrendous 12-over-par 82. "I can't explain it," Leonard lamented. "It was as though I'd forgotten everything I've ever known out there."

▲

One week, you're cleaning out the wallets of your playing partners; the next week, you're ready to toss your clubs in the pond. But don't fret. There are enough good times to make you forget about the bad ones.

As a golfer, you tend to be late for your tee time, which doesn't endear you to the rest of your foursome. You usually make up for your tardiness by showing off your sense of humor. Besides, you are the classic prankster.

After the third round of the 1999 Mercedes Championships, Fred Funk, who was in second place, borrowed the courtesy car of tourney leader David Duval. Funk returned the car in a slightly altered state. "I messed with the seats and the mirrors, turned the wipers on, moved the steering wheel, turned the heat on full blast, everything," Funk recalled. "I tried to get him worked up before we even got on the course. On the seventeenth hole, I asked him, 'By the way, how was your car this morning?' Didn't faze him." (Perhaps because Duval is a Scorpio.) The car joke backfired on Funk. He finished in a tie for fifth, eleven strokes behind the winning Duval.

You love to talk about everything and you probably have the best golf stories of anybody, although sometimes you sound like a links version of the *National Enquirer.* Since you jabber so much, you can't be without your cell phone on the golf course. This can tie things up at times, but you always know how to talk your way out of sensitive situations.

Because of your dual personality, your game is unpredictable. It's refreshing for others to play with you when you're golfing well, because that's when you tend to engage in stimulating conversation. But if you're playing lousy, chances are you'll clam up and not say a word.

▼

At the 1998 U.S. Senior Open, Hale Irwin refused to talk to the media after his first-round 77. But he was full of quotes three days later when he won. He explained to reporters that his first-round score hadn't been "worthy of conversation."

▲

The typical Gemini has a bad habit of paying too much attention to how the other players are doing rather than concentrating on his or her own golf.

▼

At the 1996 PGA Championship, Phil Mickelson had opened a three-stroke lead after 36 holes and then came out flat for the third round. "I wasn't relaxed and I didn't allow myself to play golf stress-free," he recalled. "I was so worried about what other people were doing." He shot a 74, including a double bogey when he hit a pitching wedge into a pond.

▲

Equipment

Watch your spending! Do you really need another club? You probably have more clubs than most other players. That's because one side of your personality prefers the more traditional clubs while your more adventuresome streak seeks a selection of advanced, leading-edge irons. Instead of having a matched set of clubs, you're more likely to own a set of woods by one company, irons by another, and a wedge and a putter from two other brands. You're better off with a matched set for some consistency—an attribute that you could use on the course.

Because you're such a natural-born shopper, you might want to curb your desire to buy the latest golfing gadget. Depending on the money you have to spend, you likely have a new laser yardage indicator. Try to be a little more selective in buying golf instructional tapes, golf books, and home-putting devices.

Attire

You know how to dress well, so make sure you look good because that's important to you. You view golf as a sport with class, and your attitude reflects how you dress on the course. You'll feel most comfortable if your golfwear is neither as conservative as Taurus's nor as wild as Aries's. Dress tastefully and try not to cast too critical an eye on playing partners who don't share your sense of style.

In cool weather, you love showing off one of your many sweaters. If you're like Mark Calcavecchia, you probably have one for each day of the month.

Your best colors are yellows and golds.

Don't forget your more spirited personality, which can sometimes be seen in the hat you wear. In fact, many Geminis bring more than one to the course, and change caps from the front nine to the back nine, depending on their mood.

Game Preparation

To you, the hardest part of preparing for a game is getting to the course early enough. That rarely happens, and you often find yourself rushing to change and get to the tee on time.

What a difference it would make if you arrived at the club with at least a half an hour to spare. When focused on the driving range and putting green, you display excellent coordination.

But perhaps more importantly, you need this time to figure out which game you're likely to play that day. Will you be a straight shooter with a smooth swing or a spray hitter, tacking your way down the fairway? Unfortunately for you, it's impossible to know which of your two personalities will show up on the course.

Every Gemini has his or her own way of preparing for a big game. The problem is that it's seldom the same way from one day to the next. You really could use a regular pregame routine.

▼

Says 1997 British Open champion Justin Leonard: "Everything from hitting another bag [of balls], to signing a kid's autograph, to going to a movie instead of hitting balls for another hour—it's just me finding out how to get myself playing the best I can. The right amount of relaxation, practice, goofing off, and being serious . . . I like to do all those things, so finding that right combination is something I'm looking for."

▲

Your Game

Off the Tee

Because you tend to be inconsistent in your play, the secret to your success can be in your grip. If necessary, get an expert to help you find the right grip, stance, and alignment. Your swing, especially off the tee, is different all the time— not by much, but enough to cause you to hook or slice the ball as often as you split the fairways.

The problem is typically caused by not having the proper swing thought—something that the club pro can give you. With your drives, distance is not the problem; direction is. Control that urge to kill the ball.

On the Fairway

Remember that tempo and rhythm are important to you. Stop and relax before selecting that club for the approach shot. Your tendency not to think things out ultimately costs you strokes. You can be an excellent player if you choose the right club and take a moment to figure out the best way to play the shot. You have marvelous analytical skills, but you don't use them enough.

Try taking several practice swings until you feel ready and you're seeing a picture in your mind of what you want your ball to do. Your tendency to overshoot the green usually occurs when you hurry your shot.

In the Hazard

Somehow hazards find you more easily than you find

them. For whatever reason, your ball will hit a divot or marker and make a ninety-degree turn into a bunker. Your ball seeks out water and sand as if it's a homing pigeon and they're roosts.

▼

Justin Leonard is a victim of typical Gemini luck. Gunning for a win at the 1998 Westin Texas Open, he sent a drive down the left side of the final hole—the perfect place to go for the pin. But the ball took an unexpected nasty kick into a bunker and wound up underneath the lip. He was unable to get up and down for a par that would have put him in a play-off.

▲

When you have to play the shot from the trap or rough, keep calm. Remember, one of your assets is your ability to go with the flow. You're quite good at improvising and can adjust to most situations, no matter how difficult.

It doesn't hurt to have a sense of humor when you're in a jam. Telling a self-deprecating joke about your dilemma can help you relax and ease the pressure.

On the Green

Putting can be the most frustrating part of your game. Be patient and stick to a few good putting habits taught to you by a pro. You tend not to pay a lot of attention to all the green's factors that affect the ball, such as break, speed, and condition of the grass.

You usually get over the putt and put a death grip on

the putter. Then you get so "hole conscious" that you try to jam the ball into the cup. Naturally, it doesn't work.

Says Olin Browne, winner of the 1998 Canon Greater Hartford Open, "I try to relax my hands and have a nice, loose grip. Then I take a few practice swings with a good smooth tempo."

Course Management

Even though your golf is unpredictable, you're adaptable, and this is your strongest trait. You need to play according to the conditions and make whatever adjustments are necessary.

Hale Irwin won the 1997 PGA Seniors' Championship by handling the tricky wind conditions, soggy fairways, and crusty greens. He rarely missed his target. When he did, he made sure to miss it in a safe place. It was a clinic in course management.

"I'm just playing a little bit more intelligently, picking my spots when to be aggressive and when not to," he told reporters. "Last year I gave myself carte blanche and was aggressive all the time" regardless of the conditions. In 1996, he won two tournaments playing aggressively. In 1997, when he played more shrewdly, he won nine tournaments. In 1998, using the same philosophy, Irwin won seven times, including the PGA Seniors' Championship and the U.S. Senior Open.

When you're playing your "A" game, you tend to take fewer risks and play faster. But when your game belongs on a mini-putt course, that's when you need to call on your wits to survive the round. Take a few chances if you have to; be innovative. You can find a way to overcome those days when your swing has left you and your putting stroke has betrayed you. Believe it or not, you can still finish with a decent score by being adaptable and creative to compensate for your "D" game.

Nothing seems to bother Justin Leonard, who laughs at himself more easily than he does at others. Some days he'll play in a get-me-off-the-course-before-I-hurt-myself mode but will somehow manage to pull out a good score. Other times, he's on fire, roaring back from five-shot deficits on the final day as he did at the 1997 British Open and the 1998 Players Championship.

Wagering

If your foursome is into gambling, you'll be the first to put up your money. But for your own sake, try to get to the course early so you can determine which of your two golf games has shown up. Then make your wager accordingly.

You can be a cool, calculating player who knows how to subtly psych out your opponents. You are a master at gamesmanship—especially when there are big bucks on the line. Just remember to be careful, because your antics could cause the rest of your group to shun you. Next week, you could be looking for three new playing partners.

Let's Talk

You're a natural salesperson, and there's no way to stop you from talking business on the course if you're with a client. You can be utterly charming and disconcerting and have the client eating out of your hand. If not directly in sales, you're probably in a profession that involves communication. The golf course is an excellent place to talk about the things that matter most to you.

At the 19th hole, you're a master storyteller who can disarm anyone—including the playing partner who double-bogeyed the last two holes to lose to you by a stroke.

Tee Time

Skip the early mornings—you'll definitely be running late and be totally unprepared to play. Late morning and early afternoon are best.

Poor weather conditions don't bother you because you can adapt to most any situation.

If you have a serious problem at home or at work that requires your attention, hold off on golf or you'll carry it with you on the course. And that will be bad for everyone, especially you.

Playing Partners

Birdies

ARIES: You and Aries are so energetic and extroverted, you could easily play thirty-six holes instead of eighteen—and pick up new friends along the way.

LEO: You make wonderful partners because you're both sociable players who enjoy each other's conversation and could spend hours talking in the clubhouse.

LIBRA: Both of you are easygoing and enjoy the game whether you win or lose. A charming person, especially on the golf course, Libra can help you relax.

AQUARIUS: You admire each other's intellect and energy. You make an outstanding pairing and enjoy playing together because you're both so unpredictable.

Bogeys

GEMINI: When you play with a Gemini, you have trouble getting a word in edgewise. Since you're both acid-tongued, the verbal jousting can overtake the golf game.

CANCER: You're just too different from Cancer to have a clue about this golfer. You can't deal with Cancer's supersensitivity and emotional states.

CAPRICORN: While you look at golf in a fun-loving way,

this golfer takes the game more seriously and finds you too unstructured. Beware of Capricorn's temper.

PISCES: You and Pisces just don't click because you have trouble understanding each other. Don't bet with this golfer, whose gamesmanship is just as clever as yours.

Pars

TAURUS: Your golf philosophy is considerably different than Taurus's, but you respect this golfer's consistency. Just don't become too impatient with Taurus's slow play.

VIRGO: It might be hard for you to connect with Virgo because you are such opposites. But you can learn much from Virgo, if you keep an open mind.

SCORPIO: Both you and Scorpio are fairly intuitive golfers who get along fine. Don't pull a practical joke on Scorpio, or there's likely to be a scene.

SAGITTARIUS: Both of you are party animals, and when you get together golf may take a back seat to having a good time. Just be careful not to get into a big-money bet or else the fun could vanish.

Brandel Chamblee

Nick Faldo

Bruce Lietzke

Colin Montgomerie

Loren Roberts

Scott Verplank

Billy Casper

Jerry McGee

Juli Inkster

the**cancer**golfer

sensitive

cautious

intuitive

methodical

determined

(June 22 – July 23)

Although you don't always show it on the outside, you are an extremely sensitive, emotional person who can tune in to other's emotions.

This sensitivity is definitely felt on the golf course. You pick carefully who is part of your foursome. You seek out those who are kind, thoughtful, and supportive. Because your game is dictated by emotions, you avoid partners who might be threatening in any way to the enjoyment of your game. When things get too dicey for you emotionally, you want to crawl back into your shell like your symbol, the crab.

Your sensitivity can cause you trouble on the links because you tend to take other's remarks to heart so deeply that it adversely affects your play.

▼

At the 1997 U.S. Open at Congressional, Colin Montgomerie experienced an eleven-stroke difference because of his "rabbit ears." Montgomerie hates it when someone mispronounces his name so that it sounds like the lower part of his intestine. A few drunks in the gallery picked up on that and their heckling in the second round so unnerved him that he came apart. After shooting a first-round 65, Montgomerie faltered to a 76 because he allowed himself to become unglued by the those hecklers.

▲

Because of your sensitivity, you show great empathy and sympathy to your playing partners—even if you appear on the surface to be a cool and emotionless golfer like Nick Faldo.

▼

When Faldo won the 1996 Masters because of Greg Norman's final-round collapse, Faldo gave Norman a big hug, one of the warmest gestures ever seen in golf. Although it seemed so unlike Faldo, the spontaneous embrace revealed much about the depth of his emotions.

▲

As for your game itself, you can be extremely competitive, but few realize it because you hide your emotions so well. What others don't understand is that you should never be underestimated once you've made up your mind to give the game 110 percent. Golf is important to you, and so is winning.

You refuse to give up, even if your score looks like the midday temperature in Death Valley. Let no one doubt that the competitive juices will bubble as lava-hot as ever. They just don't spill over. But in your own subtle way, you present an aura and presence which tells others that, no matter how far behind you are, they better keep looking over their shoulder.

Although you're competitive and want to win badly, you also put golf in perspective. Family is still number one with you. And even if you have a lousy day on the course, you can forget about it the moment you walk into the house and hug your spouse and kids.

▼

Bruce Lietzke, a thirteen-time winner on the PGA Tour, has entered only about ten tournaments a year since he became a family man. He says he'll keep that schedule until he's fifty-two when his daughter graduates high school. "I don't shy away from the competition and tournament play," he told reporters. "I still love it. But this is my chance to spend time with my family because golf will become important to me again in a few years, just as it was important to me before I got married and had kids."

▲

You say what you think, but sometimes you don't think about what you say. You offer quick tips and encouragement to your playing partners and supply them with plenty of gossip. Yet, sometimes the littlest distractions will stir up your bile until you lose sight of what you need to do to play good golf.

▼

Tied for the lead on the 71st hole of the 1997 U.S. Open, Colin Montgomerie had a five-foot putt for par. But instead of bearing down for one of the biggest putts of his life, he stood there angrily waiting for the noise from spectators to die down behind the 18th green. It never did. His concentration shattered, his temper rising, Montgomerie missed his par attempt and lost the Open by a stroke.

He cried all the way to the parking lot and out the front gate at Congressional. "I think that's just the emotion of the whole thing," he said later. "And I'm only human in saying that."

▲

Equipment

You're a conservative person, so your choice in equipment should be toward the traditional. Narrow your purchase to a few popular brand-name sets and then search for the most comfortable clubs you can find. Avoid all the newest-style clubs, especially those that are expensive.

Though oversized cavity-back irons still dominate the market, traditionally styled "blade" club heads are more suited for you. These irons tend to appeal to better golfers capable of "shaping" shots—making them move in flight slightly to the right or left—though there's enough forgiveness built into the forged or cast irons to benefit players with higher handicaps too.

If you're depressed or feeling hurt, you're likely to spend money unnecessarily on clubs or other golf equipment that you don't really need. That's because spending money is your way of soothing your wounds. Buy clubs when you're in a positive mood.

Because you're a pack rat, you probably have a basement or garage full of putters, woods, and golf bags and perhaps a garbage can loaded with shag balls.

Attire

You dress conventionally and for comfort. You're no fashion plate, but you're no slouch either. You'll play and feel your best in light blues, grays, and pale green. Stay away from wearing bright and gaudy colors or bold color combinations. That's not you, and they'll only distract you from your game.

Pay special attention to your shoes. Don't skimp on cheap ones. Buy top of the line, not for looks but for comfort.

Chances are you have one piece of apparel or accessory—such as a hat, sweater, or belt—that you keep touching throughout your round for security, à la Linus and his blanket. If you don't have something like that, find one and rub it often. You'll feel better, especially when you're hitting out of the rough.

Game Preparation

Your warm-up shouldn't be a practice session. This is not the time to try new equipment or work on swing changes. Instead, do a few stretching exercises and then try to find a comfortable tempo in your swing. Follow the routine of fellow Cancer Nick Faldo, who hits lots of wedges and short irons before a round and only a few woods. He starts with a mixture of chips, lobs, and sand shots, since the tempo and swing you need in the sand pretty much covers all the shots around the green.

Because you're known for having the only mobile pharmacy on the golf course, make sure you have Band-Aids, tissues, aspirin, and, most importantly, stomach medication. The stomach is typically a Cancer's weakest organ, and the slightest upset, either physically or mentally, can ruin your golf.

Your Game

Off the Tee

When you come up to the tee box, it's important for you to take several practice swings. This sets up your rhythm and allows you to concentrate on a smooth follow-through. You know that accuracy is your game, so pick a spot down the fairway that you want to hit and aim for that area. If you alter the rhythm, you'll probably top the ball. Should that happen, don't let your emotions get in the way of your next stroke. You're prone to experiencing a defeatist attitude when the hole doesn't start off well. You must accept your lousy tee shot and find a way to save par.

If you're having a bad day on the tee, forget the woods and go to a long iron.

▼

At the Senior Tour's 1998 Vantage Championship, Jerry McGee hit three-woods and long irons off the tee all week to avoid the erratic driving that had helped make it the toughest year of his career. "I don't care what anybody thinks," he told reporters. "I'm going to leave the driver in the bag."

▲

On the Fairway

Your irons are your most important weapons on the course. Because you're not a long-ball hitter off the tee, you must rely on your irons. Shorter hitters such as Nick Faldo know they have less margin for error because the John Dalys of golf get more cheap birdies on par-5's. That's why Faldo places a lot of pressure on the short game.

▼

Faldo won the 1989 Masters shooting 65 in the final round, despite hitting just nine greens in regulation. He didn't have a good ball-striking day. However, he made eight birdies, and of the nine greens he missed, he got up and down in two shots every time but once.

▲

If you're not clicking on all cylinders on the fairway, you're in big trouble. Just stay calm, practice good swing mechanics, and let your intuition direct your shots.

In the Hazard

There's no need for you to freak out when you're faced with a water hole. You're a water sign, so that pond or stream isn't necessarily your enemy.

But sand traps and bunkers are. The biggest problem for

you is the emotional stress that wracks your body when you're in a hazard. Don't beat yourself up over a bad shot. It's only a game with friends. You know how to get out of this predicament, so reach down inside, find that competitive spirit, and loft that ball onto the green.

On the Green

Your putting is solid and reliable but generally not very spectacular beyond twenty feet. You like to stroke long putts at a speed that minimizes the chances of the dreaded three-putt. As a result, you don't record a lot of birdies or bogeys.

You need to spend more time reading the green. Squat down to get a better perspective of the green and its undulation to determine whether it's going to break right or left. Cup your eyes to narrow your field of vision so you can see your line better. Don't let others hurry you or else you'll get rattled. Once you've read the green, put everything out of your mind and stroke the ball.

Loren Roberts, after winning the 1995 Nestlé Invitational, disclosed that he putted with "my eyes out of focus and my brain in neutral."

Course Management

Your key to a successful game is methodical playing.

Don't let anyone force you to play faster or slower than you want to. Your body has a unique rhythm, and if you orient your play to that rhythm, you should shoot well.

▼

Nick Faldo has always played his best when, as he himself admits, "I was mechanical and boring."

▲

When you're faced with a difficult lie, you should rely more on your intuitive skill. It's like having an extra club in your bag. It will serve you well.

However, Cancer, you're your own worst enemy at times. Because you tend to be somewhat insecure, you don't take chances on difficult shots. You lack trust in your own ability and rarely see yourself as the best player. While your game is good, it could be outstanding with some attempts to reach beyond what you think you can do. Dig deep down inside yourself and call on that competitive spirit that's raring to get out.

▼

Fire yourself up like Nick Faldo has done to win six majors: "Do it on the day. Do it when it matters most. Do it when it's absolutely nerve-racking. Do it when it's all you can do to take a breath. The screws get tighter. And the great ones find a way to do it on the day."

▲

Wagering

Because you worry a lot and have a stomach that acts up every so often, you're better off not betting on the course. Besides, you're not a good gambler and you don't do well under pressure. Secondly, you don't like to take financial risks, however small.

But the flip side is that you want to be included and will feel uncomfortable if you're left out. Therefore, if the others want to wager, join in—as long as the stakes aren't too high and the betting game is simple. Under no circumstances bet more than you can afford to lose. If you do, you'll be unhappy long after the game is over.

You have a heart of gold, and your kindness would never allow you take advantage of others by employing psych-out tactics or other forms of gamesmanship. Unfortunately, you can easily fall prey to your playing partners' good-natured taunts, causing you to miss an easy putt. Although it's not in your nature, joke back or try to ignore them.

Let's Talk

Friends and acquaintances know you are a wealth of knowledge, so you probably are asked your opinion on many issues. Be careful, because you can get passionate about certain subjects that are better discussed in a place other than the golf course. Also, avoid your tendency to offer personal advice or get too involved in someone else's problems. And that goes for you on or off the course.

Tee Time

Your sign is ruled by the moon, which means you're a night person, not a morning person. Therefore, you tend to play much better if you're teeing off in late morning or in the afternoon.

Your golfing performance isn't much affected by humidity or rainy conditions, although you seem to get your best scores in cool weather.

Playing Partners

Birdies

TAURUS: You have a lot in common with Taurus. You both play conservatively and tend to share the same beliefs on a wide range of topics.

LEO: Although quite different from you, Leo can help you enjoy golf to its fullest and ease your insecurities simply through his or her enthusiastic cheerleading.

VIRGO: This golfer is usually in tune with you and appreciates your determined, methodical play. You both tend to go out of the way to help the other with golf tips.

PISCES: You both share many of the same traits—you're gentle, caring, and sensitive. Pisces is always seeking advice, and you love to give it.

Bogeys

ARIES: Emotionally, you don't understand each other and don't play golf the same way. A bad shot by you can elicit a negative comment from Aries which could adversely affect your play.

GEMINI: This extrovert sooner or later says something that you take personally. It festers in you and can upset your game, your day, and your stomach.

SAGITTARIUS: Sagittarius's fun-loving approach to the game can be quite distracting for you. Sag has a way of making you feel insecure.

AQUARIUS: You two are definite opposites. You'll never understand this golfer's unorthodox style in life and golf. Aquarius might exploit your insecurities on the course.

Pars

CANCER: Playing with another Cancer is okay. However, you must remember that you both can easily become overly sensitive, and this could affect your golf.

LIBRA: When carrying on conversations, Libra often is on your wavelength. But this golfer may bug you too much for advice on the game and on life.

SCORPIO: This golfer can bring out the competitive juices in you. But Scorpio's intensity and gambling can make you feel a bit uneasy.

CAPRICORN: On the golf course Capricorn and you can be quite compatible. However, this player does have a temper, which can be distracting for you.

Brad Faxon

Billy Mayfair

Hugh Baiocchi

Doug Sanders

Betsy King

Dottie Pepper

Colleen Walker

the**leo**golfer

self-confident

risk-taking

forceful

enthusiastic

charismatic

(July 24 – August 23)

The sun rules Leo and shines for all to see. You, Leo, have that something extra in your personality that warms all those around you. Your friends and acquaintances seek you out because they know golfing with you will be a special day on the course.

When you're playing, your charisma glistens like a finely polished putter. You're always cheering on your playing partners, giving them emotional boosts, urging them to try shots that they otherwise would be afraid to attempt. No one doubts your sincerity or encouragement. Everyone loves your ardor for life and golf.

▼

For enthusiasm on the course, Dottie Pepper leads the LPGA. She's their most volatile personality. That was never more evident than at the 1998 Solheim Cup, when the Americans beat Team Europe 16-12. When she wasn't winning all four of her matches, Dottie was acting like an overzealous cheerleader, pumping her fists and hugging her teammates, much to the annoyance of the Europeans. Dottie's exuberance and spirit inspired her entire team.

▲

The symbol for you is the lion, and it shows in your manner and grooming. Female Leos often have long hair that's perfectly groomed, while males likely sport trimmed facial hair.

You can be generous to a fault in offering your friends money and advice. With your strong sense of confidence, you work hard to prove yourself to others. All these positive qualities can turn to negatives if done to the extreme. You can be overpowering and very unforgiving to those who aren't up to your standards. You need to guard against becoming the most pompous player on the course.

You tend to be a streaky player. When you're hot, you're smoking; when you're not, you're really bad. You often go through stretches when you've put it all together and nobody can beat you. Then, inexplicably, everybody, including the ball shagger, can beat you. Billy Mayfair is like that.

If you were to chart Mayfair's golfing success, it would look like a profile of the Rocky Mountains—all peaks and valleys. He was 30th on the PGA Tour money list in 1993, 113th the next year, 2nd in 1995, followed by 55th and 97th, before finishing 16th in 1998, which was a very strange year. In his first five tournaments of 1998, Mayfair's best finish was 25th. But he beat Tiger Woods in a play-off to win the Nissan Open and finished 2nd the next week at the Doral-Ryder Open. Then he went back into a funk. In his next eleven tournaments, Mayfair missed the cut four times and finished no better than 31st. But then he won the Buick Open and finished 7th the following week at the PGA Championship.

You also tend to tinker a lot with your swing and other mechanics of the game. You probably keep making a slight change in posture at address or a correction of the hands at the top of the swing. But you're never really comfortable without making those adjustments.

As Hall of Famer and two-time U.S. Women's Open champion Betsy King once explained, "You can visualize hitting a 250-yard draw all you want, but unless you have the swing mechanics to produce that shot, it won't happen.

"For me, the mental side has always been pretty constant. I think well on the golf course, so it's just a question of getting my swing mechanics straight."

▲

Equipment

Your desire to be among the best golfers on the course means you need top-quality clubs. Custom clubs are the only way to go, damn the expense. You won't be happy with anything less. Talk to your club pro about a fitting session that will help you determine the club design that is right for your swing. Spend time with a club fitter and discuss how changing club length, as part of an overall custom-fit design, can improve your game.

Don't abandon your favorite putter and switch to one of those fancy new ones made from soft carbon steel or manganese bronze. Assuming you're nailing those ten-footers, stay with the putter you have. However, if you're uncharacteristically missing putts you used to make, consider a change.

Go ahead and indulge yourself by buying trendy-looking accessories, especially ones that you can show off. You should probably be using a bag in a striking color of the finest leather. Your head covers and umbrella should be multicolored and totally different from everyone else's.

Attire

Hopefully, you have a spouse or friend who helps keep you in check in your choice of clothes, because you can border on the outrageous.

Nevertheless, you're most comfortable wearing loud or bright colors such as gold, orange, red, and yellow. You're a proud person who can act classy in clothes that would make others look foolish. It's your style, and it works for you. Your playing partners are often in awe of what you wear. There's a fine line, however, between looking like your clothes come from Tommy Bahama and not Ringling Brothers.

▼

No one on the PGA Tour was more of a fashion plate than Doug Sanders. His closet—bigger than most bedrooms—was crammed with clothes of every color of the rainbow and shoes to match. His trademark attire on the course included a sweater, shirt, pants, socks, and patent leather shoes all of the same color, including lavender, lime, and coral.

One of Sanders's *GQ* moments on the course occurred during the 1966 Masters, when he played the final round in tangerine-colored attire, from spikes to sweater.

▲

Game Preparation

You're a golfer with enormous willpower and a huge reserve of hope. You never look back, only forward, and therefore you prepare mentally by packing your brain with positive thoughts.

In your pregame practice, hit no more than a couple dozen balls and get a feel for what is working. Don't overload on your swing thoughts. They might change from week to week, depending on what is or isn't working for you. Then stay focused on one or two swing keys.

If you didn't do well the week before, convince yourself that this round will be better than ever. You probably were out at the practice range during the week, whacking balls to the point of exhaustion. You're not afraid of hard work to achieve winning results, especially if golf is your passion.

Use your last few warm-up swings to hit the shots you expect to need on the opening holes because you like to get off to a good start.

Since you're not too fond of exercise, find time to do some stretching movements before you hit your first practice shot.

Your Game

Off the Tee

Blasting drives is the favorite part of your game, even though you don't necessarily hit the ball that far. You like tee-ing off because everybody is watching you, and you have great confidence in your swing. The ball usually rockets out straight and true.

You like to set the standard for each hole, so when you're pleased with your drive, encourage your playing partners to do even better. If you send a slice sailing into the woods, don't make excuses. Instead, urge the others not to follow your lead—but only on that hole. You know you'll get another chance at the next hole. Leos don't look back, only forward.

On the Fairway

You have the makeup of a risk-taker, so go after birdies the way a hungry lion goes after a zebra—with gusto. So what if a creek or bunker is guarding the green? Your brain is wired with enough positive thoughts to convince you that your ball will sail over trouble and land in birdie territory.

In fact, don't be shy about announcing to your playing part-ners that you're gunning for a bird.

In the Hazard

Although you have the heart of a world-class golfer, you probably don't have the exceptional skills of those on the tour, which means you're often waging war in Bunker Hell.

Being a Leo, you should graciously accept your plight and try to scramble out of trouble as quickly as possible. But don't rush your shot. You need to take the time to analyze the situation and come up with the right shot or you'll spend more time in the sand and water than a Florida tourist.

On the Green

If your friends took the advice of the late instructor Har-vey Penick—"have dinner with good putters"—you'd be invited out every night. Putting is your forte, your salvation, your rescuer from an otherwise so-so round.

You're a natural-born putter who likely wows your play-ing partners with your greensmanship. Just don't get bogged down in putting mechanics. Rely on your ability to see the line of a putt and hit it at the proper speed. In fact, you're so good at putting, you can spend the least amount of time on it during practice.

▼

Brad Faxon, one of the PGA Tour's best putters, needed only 103 putts during the week when he won the Freeport-McDermott Classic in 1997. "I didn't hit one practice putt this week except before I went out to play my rounds," he told reporters. "That's pretty typical.

"Putting is attitude more than anything. There are no absolutes in putting—except that all the great putters are confident. It's more important to be decisive than it is to be correct."

▲

Even you are impressed with how well your putter performs. But watch yourself or else you'll get too confident and blow an easy two-footer, leaving you an embarrassed blush as bright as your clothes.

Course Management

While others may play the percentages, you are a risk taker and also like to show off that you can make the impossible shot.

You enjoy playing golf on the edge, trying the impossible behind-the-tree, over-the-bunker approach that drops directly behind the pin and spins back. But you need to find a happy medium with your course management. Too much risk and your gambling, shortcut tee shot fails to make the dogleg, or the pin-hunting approach flies the green and suddenly you're posting a snowman on your scorecard.

Yes, it's true you don't like to look back, but there are times when you should replay in your mind all those shots you tried in similar circumstances that failed. You need to know the difference between calculated risks and reckless ones.

Wagering

You love to gamble and you can't stand to play if a wager isn't involved in your friendly game. With money on the line, you have even more reason to bear down and play an intense round.

▼

During a practice round at the 1994 British Open, Brad Faxon, Davis Love III, Corey Pavin, and Ben Crenshaw each put up $1,000. The golfer who could play eighteen holes without a bogey would win the pot. Faxon played a flawless round and walked off with three grand in his pocket. Days later, Faxon came in seventh—his best finish ever at the British Open.

▲

Although betting on the course can get your heart pumping, don't get too fired up or it can adversely affect your golf.

▼

During the biennial battle for the Solheim Cup, Dottie Pepper admitted that she can get too intense. "I hit two clubs farther than usual, that's how pumped up I get. It's probably equal to a Zantac or two."

▲

You like raising the stakes, especially by coming up with side bets on every other hole. But you need to be careful.

Your overconfidence could get you into trouble and by the end of the game you could be walking off the course with a thin wallet.

You're not big on gamesmanship just to win a bet. In fact, you think less of a playing partner if he or she tries to psych you out. You believe that a golf game is won or lost by how well you hit the ball, not by how cleverly you play mind games.

Let's Talk

You're never at a loss for words. Knowing the right time to say the right thing is a skill you were born with.

You generally take control of the conversation, so if it's appropriate to bring up business on the course, do it. Otherwise save it for the clubhouse or another time. However, there are times when you need to blurt out what's on your mind because you can't hold it in. Your boldness and daring in saying something out of the blue to get someone's attention can be just the thing to snag that account or resolve a problem.

Tee Time

Since the sun rules you, playing at midday is the best time for you. If you're stuck with an early-morning tee time, chances are you'll shoot much better on the back nine.

You tend to peak throughout the summer, when the sun is the highest in the sky. The hotter the temperature, the hotter your game. You simply won't wilt in the heat and humidity. But if it's cold and blustery, the only birdie you'll likely get is a postgame turkey sandwich.

Playing Partners

Birdies

ARIES: You two like to play fast, high-energy golf and thrive on each other's enthusiasm. You're both notorious for springing for drinks or lunch after a round, especially if you win that big wager.

GEMINI: You make wonderful partners because you're both sociable players who enjoy swapping funny and wild golf stories. You feed off each other on and off the course. Besides, Gemini listens to your golf tips.

LIBRA: Although you two have entirely different approaches to the game, you nonetheless make a good pairing. You just click together, perhaps because you have so much to talk about and laugh about—and bet on.

SAGITTARIUS: You enjoy Sag's energy, enthusiasm, and optimistic outlook on life because those are traits that you possess. Here's a golfer who can out-talk you and make you laugh.

Bogeys

TAURUS: Although you're fairly compatible, you both have strong personalities that can at times clash. Your forceful nature and Taurus's obstinacy can cause you some uncomfortable moments.

LEO: A foursome can take only one Leo. Two lions in the same pack could create royal battles unless one of you backs down or keeps that tongue in check—an unlikely scenario for a typical Leo.

VIRGO: There's just too much analyzing from this restrained golfer. Virgo can slow your game down so much it will aggravate you for the whole round.

AQUARIUS: There's something about this golfer's swagger and bulldog determination that gets under your skin. You like to be praised for a good shot, but you won't get it from Aquarius, even if you made a hole in one.

Pars

CANCER: You can benefit from this golfer's cautious, methodical approach to the game on days your risk taking isn't paying off. However, you can get quickly tired of Cancer's mood swings.

SCORPIO: Your personalities can blend well on the course, but beware of Scorpio's sharp tongue, which can unwittingly whiplash your big ego.

CAPRICORN: There can be a subtle battle about who has the best clubs, bag, balls, and clothes. But if you can get past that, Capricorn can make a pleasant playing partner.

PISCES: This gentle golfer is so accommodating that he or she would be your caddie if you asked. Pisces makes a good audience for you, but not necessarily a good opponent.

Raymond Floyd

Lee Janzen

Skip Kendall

Larry Mize

Arnold Palmer

Scott Simpson

Jeff Sluman

Tom Watson

Bernhard Langer

Isao Aoki

Larry Nelson

Jane Blalock

Louise Suggs

the**virgo**golfer

analytical

deliberate

down-to-earth

practical

disciplined

(August 24 – September 23)

Probably the most diligent sign of the zodiac, Virgo is the brains of the astrological chart. Your strength lies in your ability to analyze any situation and come up with a solution—and it shows on the golf course. No matter where your ball is—under the lip of a bunker or on the edge of a steep bank—you'll figure out the correct shot. However, executing that shot is another matter, unless you're Raymond Floyd, the quintessential Virgo golfer.

On difficult shots, you don't panic or get too worked up. You confront the fear head-on and try to work out a physical solution to the problem.

▼

Says Floyd: "I don't try to pep-talk my way into a good shot by saying, 'You can do it.' That's self-delusion. Nor do I minimize the importance of the shot. There are golfers who tell themselves, 'It's not a big deal—either you pull it off or you don't.' I say, if that's your attitude, you're not much of a competitor."

▲

If you're a typical Virgo, you're probably the slowest among your foursome because you're so deliberate. But fortunately, it's not because you suffer from a bad case of indecision. You just want all the facts before coming up with a conclusion. And once that decision is made, you act on it, for better or worse.

If it's for the worse, you tend to get angry, but you won't necessarily show it. The impractical Virgos get ticked off at themselves and end up playing tighter, which throws off their rhythm and flow. The anger becomes upsetting and distracting. If you react like this, your ire will play havoc with your analytical mind and cause you to criticize and overanalyze everything you do. You'll start thinking about the mechanical flaws in your swing and try to correct them. The result: You'll very likely play worse.

The practical Virgo finds a way to divert that anger by blaming the weather, the course architect, the astrological forecast—anything but himself or herself.

▼

Some of the world's top Virgo golfers have developed idiosyncratic ways of deflecting the rage that bubbles up within them after a bad shot. Arnold Palmer and Bernhard Langer tend to blame their clubs, frequently switching from one set to another and banishing the offending implements to a dark basement. Langer has been known to soak his clubs in a barrel of water overnight as punishment for their betrayal. He did that the week he won the first of his two Masters.

▲

Because you're an earth sign, you enjoy golf for reasons other than just the sport of it. You have an enduring love of nature and always take a few moments on the course to gaze at the trees, flowers, and landscape.

Equipment

Whether you're a casual golfer or an avid one, you should spend a lot of time choosing the right clubs. Read up on all the latest technology and talk to your friends and the club pro to get their input.

Because you're so analytical, don't pick out clubs according to feel. Instead, study all the factors—lie angle, length, shaft flex, shaft material, grip size, swing weight, overall weight, and clubhead design. Once you've gathered all the information, make your decision and hunt for the best buy in your price range.

Attire

Your conservative nature dictates the clothes you wear. Because you're very conscious of maintaining a good image, you'll feel most comfortable in solid colors, especially indigo or violet, which are your strongest hues.

Don't bother trying to look flashy. Instead, project a traditional, immaculate appearance and avoid wearing jewelry or fancy logoed accessories because that's not your style.

Female Virgos tend to wear little makeup, while their male counterparts typically sport closely cropped hair. To you, clothes don't make the golfer. In fact, Virgos who are occasional golfers often play on municipal courses in their sneakers and clothes that didn't come from a golf shop.

Game Preparation

Your real preparation should begin when you sit down for breakfast. Eating healthily is especially important. If your body isn't charged with a good breakfast, your golf will suffer.

Because you're always trying to improve your game, arrive at the course with plenty of time to loosen up and work on your swing and putting. Also, question golfers as they come off the course. How fast are the greens? How soggy is the fairway? How difficult are the pin placements? You should pay attention to the smallest details and file away all the information for later use.

It never hurts to seek out pros or players with lower handicaps and try to pick up golfing tips.

Said Raymond Floyd about fellow Virgo Arnold Palmer: "He was my hero. To see him with those late charges, tugging at those pants, that was something. I never took a golf lesson from Arnold, but I learned a million things from him. Back in the mid-1960s, I played a lot of practice rounds with Arnold. I searched for him at tournaments. I'd find out when he was practicing—daylight or dark, I didn't care. 'Arnold, where do you like to drive it on this hole?' I'd ask. That one question would open up a world of explanation. I watched the way he handled the courses and handled his game. I tried to emulate his aggressive style of play."

▲

If you're an avid golfer, you should practice at least once a week at the range, making slight adjustments in your quest to find the perfect swing. Practice isn't boring to you. It's fun.

On golf day, try to be the first one ready. Have your equipment in order and be prepared for the elements, including an extra towel, gloves, and, if necessary, a sweater.

You should set a new goal for yourself before each round. It can be as simple as beating your playing partners, shaving two putts off your last score, or picking up a couple more pars than you had the previous week.

Your Game

Off the Tee

You never like to be the first one to tee off. In fact, given the choice you'd prefer being last so you can study how the conditions are affecting the drives. When it's your turn, wait until it's perfectly quiet, because you don't like any kind of distractions.

Despite your systematic mind, there should be no conscious thinking about all the motions involved in making your swing while you're teeing off. There's just not enough time. Try taking several practice swings to program yourself.

Then stand up to the ball and make your swing without having those destructive swing thoughts get in the way.

On the Fairway

Because of your analytical skills, you have the ability to pick the right club for each shot, even if you don't always hit it exactly to where you want.

You're best suited for the more conservative, classic style of play favored over the years by many of the best players. They don't try to kill the ball all the time. They play their best when they swing using about 85 percent of their strength. They control the distance and maneuver the ball better. In most cases, you should do the same thing.

One other thing to remember: If you're too cautious, your shot will usually fall short. The trick for you is to know when to go for broke and when to take it easy.

In the Hazard

With all the practice you do beforehand, getting out of the sand trap isn't that difficult. If you have an extremely difficult lie, accept it and play smart. This is not the time for careless, high-risk shots.

If it doesn't go well, avoid trying to overanalyze what went wrong. At least nobody will hear you whine or complain about the poor shot; that's not in your nature.

On the Green

This is your game. All your practice pays off here. You can scope the green with the skill of a land surveyor and visualize the path the ball should—and usually does—take.

▼

Arnold Palmer likes to tell this story about Raymond Floyd's psychological approach to putting: "Once Raymond hit a long putt into the hole and his playing partner says, 'Man, that was great. How did you do that?' And Raymond says, 'I saw a pair of railroad tracks going toward the hole and there was a locomotive going down the tracks. Didn't you smell the smoke?'"

▲

Don't be rushed. You need to analyze the data. But don't fall into a common Virgo trap of paralysis by analysis or you'll wind up with a bad case of the yips, like that suffered years ago by Bernhard Langer.

Course Management

You take a businesslike approach when you play. In your head is a plan for how to attack each hole, when you think you should lay up, and when you think it's worth a risk.

It's important for you to follow a preshot routine that includes a quick assessment of what you want to accomplish by positioning yourself behind the ball and determining your line of flight.

"I visualize the shot I need to play for the given conditions," says Raymond Floyd. "I actually 'see' the ball fly toward the green and land near the flagstick. Then I continue my preshot routine with my proper alignment to my target, and my waggle to get me comfortable. Only then am I prepared to execute the swing and make a well-played shot."

▲

One of the biggest mistakes a Virgo can make is to lose sight of his or her goal for the day. Sometimes you can get caught up in all the golf bets and take unnecessary chances that throw you off your game plan.

In 1966, Arnold Palmer was so intent on smashing the record for the lowest score ever in the U.S. Open that he lost sight of his original goal—to win the championship. As a result of his wayward thinking, Arnie got a little reckless. He blew a seven-shot lead over the final nine holes and wound up losing to Billy Casper in one of the greatest collapses ever in a major tournament. Before his downfall, Palmer assumed he would break Ben Hogan's record. "That was my mistake," Arnie ruefully admitted later.

▲

Although you might be slow and deliberate, that doesn't mean you shouldn't be aggressive on the course. During the height of his career, when he won seven majors between 1958 and 1964, Arnold Palmer displayed an awesome swash-buckling style where he shot at pins, escaped from trouble, and often went for broke. Yet for all his playing-on-the-edge appearance, he knew exactly what he was doing on every shot. He was simply quick to analyze the situation.

Tom Watson is another great Virgo golfer who, on the sur-face, seems to go against the sign's characteristics. For years he has attacked the course with the intensity and smugness of an overly confident linksman. But beneath that arrogant exterior, there's the prudent strategist analyzing all the possibilities before quickly making up his mind.

Wagering

You're not a big bettor. But because you're a polite and considerate person, you go along with whatever the other players want. Most of the time you come out ahead. That's because you're even-tempered and you don't show your emotions. This gives you an edge in wagering. You do better with betting games that don't pit one team against another. Your success has always been attributed to your own efforts.

▼

Raymond Floyd would rather play a practice round alone than play one without some money on the line. But it isn't the chance to win money, he explains. "If money had been my motive for anything I don't think I'd ever have been worth a flip. I'm not gambling on the golf course. I'm practicing winning. When you're going one-on-one, there's no second, third, or fourth. You have to win."

▲

No one can accuse you of gamesmanship. You have too much respect for yourself and others to rely on head games to win. Just laugh off any attempts by a playing partner to try to psych you out.

Let's Talk

You're a workaholic, and your job is never far from your thoughts. You tend to start the business talk at the first tee, but it's best if you don't use the course for business. Everybody needs recreation and time to get away from the daily grind, and you should enjoy these nonbusiness hours. Of course, there are exceptions, but think twice before bringing up details of that unsigned contract. There's always the 19th hole, as well as tomorrow, to discuss these issues.

You're not the easiest person to get to know because you hide your feelings well, so use this time on the course to let your playing partners see the real you.

Tee Time

Virgos typically play the best golf in the afternoon. You need time to get ready, however, so plan on arriving at the course ahead of schedule. Besides, you want to have the opportunity to talk with golfers who've already played so you can have a clearer picture of the conditions.

Inclement weather and temperature extremes don't hamper your game because you're prepared to deal with whatever Mother Nature throws at you.

Playing Partners

Birdies

TAURUS: You're both committed to playing a good, solid game of golf. Your cool, calm attitudes and analytical skills make for excellent partners.

VIRGO: You two can analyze each other's shots endlessly (sometimes boring your playing partners). You enjoy playing together because you have great respect for each other.

SCORPIO: You both are impressed with the other's balanced, disciplined approach to the game. You're not likely to talk a lot to each other, but you have an unspoken bond.

CAPRICORN: Here's a competitor who can bring out the best in you without getting you uptight. You both share the same work ethic, and you each know the other is always prepared.

Bogeys

ARIES: Aries's enthusiasm tends to rub you the wrong way. Although Aries can respect your mental and physical skills, this golfer is just too fast and aggressive for you.

GEMINI: You two are as different from each other as a hickory-shafted mashie and a titanium pitching wedge. Your restrained manner and Gemini's unpredictable nature aren't a good mix for you.

LEO: This golfer's strong "take control" nature could upset your game, especially when Leo says "hurry up." You don't particularly like Leo's overbearing personality.

SAGITTARIUS: You aren't a spontaneous, energetic person the way Sagittarius is. You can easily get distracted by Sag's jokes and horseplay.

Pars

CANCER: This golfer is usually in tune with you and appreciates your brainy, diligent play. You might get a little annoyed by Cancer's efforts to get you to open up.

LIBRA: You enjoy Libra's expressive, easygoing manner on and off the course. But Libra's desire for high-stakes gambling can be a turnoff for you.

AQUARIUS: Aquarius is more of a cerebral, conservative golfer who often thinks like you do. However, you have trouble understanding Aquarius's eccentricities and impulsive behavior.

PISCES: Although you don't have a lot in common, you two tend to get along okay. However, try to stay cool if Pisces tries to play any head games with you.

John Cook

Fred Couples

Ernie Els

George Archer

Gil Morgan

Chi Chi Rodriguez

J. C. Snead

Kermit Zarley

Beth Daniel

Laura Davies

Se Ri Pak

Kelly Robbins

Annika Sorenstam

Kathy Whitworth

the**libra**golfer

perceptive

image-conscious

charming

expressive

balanced

(September 24 − October 23)

Like Libra's sign of the scales, you look for balance in your home, work, and play. Because you have an incredible perspective on life, you don't get too wrapped up in golf, believing there are so many more things that are just as important or fun for you.

No matter what the situation, you can see both sides of nearly any issue. You find a reason for everything, including the cause for every bad swing or putt.

You're an easygoing person who may lack the energy or fire to attack the course. You're not the most competitive golfer on the links, although you always try your best.

For you, the fun of playing is good enough. Shooting par, of course, would make it much better, but a low score isn't crucial for you to have a great time on the links. Because of this attitude and your lack of a killer instinct, it may appear to some that you haven't reached your full potential as a golfer. But in reality you've put the game in perspective. Some days on the course are better than others.

Says Chi Chi Rodriguez, "You know, when I lose, I don't mind. And when I win, I sort of feel like I'm used to it."

Whether you score triple digits or shoot par, you certainly enjoy the game. And your playing partners certainly enjoy you. Your wit and charm on the course can ease the pain of anyone's double bogey. Like Chi Chi, you keep your foursome loose with clever one-liners, delightful repartee, and funny schtick.

After a birdie, Chi Chi will do his celebration sword dance, in which he uses his putter to fence with an imaginary golf demon. Then he impales the hole, wipes off the imaginary blood with a handkerchief, and thrusts his "sword" into an imaginary scabbard before striding off the green.

A typical Chi Chi quip: "You know what I did one year? I was so nervous I drank a fifth of rum before I played. I shot the happiest 83 of my life."

You have a quality about you that makes you everyone's favorite. Your engaging personality and winning smile are as appealing as back-to-back birdies.

▼

Says Ernie Els about fellow Libra Fred Couples, "If I can't win, I root for him. Most of us guys feel the same way. He's the most popular player out here, inside and out-side the ropes. He goes halfway around the world, and people love him."

Couples is flattered. "If fans like me, maybe it's because I don't get too high or low out there," he said. "I try not to show anybody up and not embarrass the sport.

"I think they know that, hopefully, I'm not going to do anything really stupid, other than a stupid shot here and there. I mean, I'm not going to drink and drive or cheat or get into a fight or any of that kind of stuff."

▲

You hate being alone and like to be around people. In fact, you'd never play a round of golf by yourself. If you had to, you'd wait an hour or two at the starter's shack to be the fourth in a group of strangers.

Knowing it's virtually impossible to play a perfect round, you can accept the fact that you're going to hit some bad shots. The trick is not getting too upset over the wayward ball or fretting about a previous shot.

▼

Ernie Els says he appreciates Fred Couples's attitude. "Once he hits a shot, it's gone. If it's bad, so what?

There's nothing he can do about it. I think that's great."

John Cook said he used to verbally abuse himself on the course. One day while he was home recovering from a hand injury, he was watching golf on television. He noticed that temper tantrums were crippling some of the players. After that, Cook said, "I got myself to reflect on more positives than negatives."

▲

Equipment

With you, it's the look. While it's important to have clubs that fit, be aware that the image they project is also subconsciously a big priority for you. Whether or not you have an unlimited budget, you won't really be satisfied until you find a way to own the most expensive, or at least the most impressive, brand of clubs on the market. Even if you can't play like a pro, you try to look like one.

You don't need to be too picky when it comes to the type of shaft and size of the clubhead. But feel should be important and that, combined with looks, will determine what clubs you choose.

As for accessories, you want them to enhance your image as a classy golfer. If you can afford it, go ahead and spend hundreds on a top-of-the-line bag. Make everything from your wood covers to your umbrella reflect your impeccable taste.

Attire

You are definitely the best-dressed golfer on the course, but not the most flamboyant. You exude style in your choice of clothes and in the way you carry yourself. Your strong features give you a presence that is rarely seen in other signs.

When you walk onto the course, try to look like you just stepped out of a *Golf Digest* apparel ad. Don't wear signature series of golfwear if the logo is very large because the Libra mind considers that tacky. You want people to see the name of the brand, but without having the logo appear too obvious.

You lust after luxury styling and fabrics with new weaves. If you want to look and play your best, dress in subtle colors of pale blues, greens, and pastels. For slacks or shorts, try to match your top with a complementary color.

To accent your classy look, wear a wide-brimmed hat rather than a cap or a visor.

Game Preparation

Because you tend to examine every situation in detail, you sometimes have trouble making decisions. Golf is no exception. Use your time on the practice tee and putting green to see what clubs and parts of your game seem to be working best on that particular day. Then develop your strategy for the course and stick with it.

It's wise for you to practice with someone else, whether it's a playing partner or the club pro. You need that feedback from a person who'll give you constructive criticism—

as well as praise when warranted—before you reach the first tee.

Take a few minutes after you practice to make sure that your equipment is clean and you look your best.

Your Game

Off the Tee

Your drives say more about your intellect than about your strength. You're much better hitting the ball for accuracy rather than distance.

It's important that you trust your woods and your swing. If you don't, your drives will suffer. But, hey, you bought the best woods you could afford, right? And you've practiced with them, so you should have the confidence you need to hit those nice tee shots. As you address the ball, visualize the feel and sound that you experienced when you hit your best drive ever. There's no reason why you can't repeat that time and time again.

On the Fairway

Libras tend to have a smooth, unhurried swing. But you have a bad habit of hitting ten straight shots and then shanking one. However, you're resourceful. You won't beat yourself—unless you get too aggressive. When par is a good score, you're a great player.

▼

Ernie Els, winner of two U.S. Opens, plays a control game when mistake-free golf is paramount to success. At the 1996 and 1997 Opens, he scored a bogey or worse on just 23 of 144 holes (16 percent).

▲

In the Hazard

You tend to find hazards at the most inopportune time. Water and sand are like magnets to you, especially on the later holes. Play those last few holes with less valor and more discretion.

▼

Fred Couples lost the 1998 GTE Byron Nelson Classic on the finishing holes when he landed in bunkers on No. 12 and No. 16. Then he rinsed his tee shot on the 173-yard par-3 17th for a triple bogey. A month earlier, he splashed a six-iron on the 13th at the Masters to seal his doom.

▲

While you're walking to your ball, decide how you're going to play the shot. If you tarry too long, you'll likely get flustered.

On the Green

There are three ways you can become a good putter: practice, practice, practice. Take lessons and try different putters, because this is the place where you can shave a few strokes off your game.

For the LPGA's Kelly Robbins, putting used to be the part
of her game that let her down. Before the 1998 season,
Kelly intensified her putting sessions with her father, Steve
Robbins, who serves as her swing coach. She putted on
practically every smooth-rolling carpet offered to her in
basements and indoor golf centers back home in Michi-
gan. The practices paid off. Kelly won the first tournament
of the year, making fifteen birdies on the weekend. She
finished the year seventeenth on the money list.

Putting is all mental with you. You either have the confidence to knock in that five-footer or you'll be changing putters
more often than Michelle McGann changes hats.

In 1998 LPGA star Laura Davies was so frustrated with
her putting that she went through twenty-two putters
during the season. She wound up 154th in the tour's putting rankings with an average of 30.77 putts per round,
an ugly total that neutralized her usual strengths.

▲

Course Management

It's important that you don't do too much thinking while

you weigh the advantages and disadvantages of every club choice you make. Speed up your play and take less time with your decisions so you can get into a rhythm.

If you're in doubt over what club to use, take more club. You don't have the strongest swing and tend to be somewhat timid on the short shots.

Your best bet is to create a plan in advance about how you'll handle the course and then follow that plan.

Normally, you're as cool as they come. You're unbelievably patient and never rush. Your blood pressure tends to be the same whether it's the 2nd hole or the 17th. However, you can get rattled when you go from cruise control to damage control. A few bad holes in a row can send your brain frantically searching for an answer to stem your poor play. But usually, the harder you try, the worse your golf becomes.

At the 1992 U.S. Open, Gil Morgan became the only golfer ever to reach double digits under par in the tournament's history when he was 12 under after forty-three holes. But he hit a couple of loose shots and couldn't convert the key putt that would have stabilized him. He fell apart and finished eight shots behind winner Tom Kite. Said Morgan ruefully, "I guess my parachute had a hole in it."

To cure this all-too-typical Libra problem, you need to develop a contrived form of amnesia. In other words, forget what happened on the last hole. Don't make how you play the current hole dependent upon the results of the previous one. Focus solely on the present, making one shot at a time. What happened earlier shouldn't matter.

Wagering

Let's face it. You're always looking for easy money, so you like to wager on the game. You're a fairly consistent golfer, and a little gambling appeals to you. Not one to wager solely on your own skill, you like betting games that pit one team against another.

When it comes to gamesmanship, you're one of the best. You know what joke to crack that appears funny and innocent but can throw off an opponent just enough to miss that two-footer. Sometimes your antics or quips themselves can unwittingly cause one of the players to lose his or her concentration.

Let's Talk

You're a master of social interaction. You can talk about anything at any time, most of it laced with a touch of humor. If the discussion turns serious, you're quick to understand both sides of the issue.

It's probably smart if you don't bring up business or heavy subjects while you're playing. Golf is for fun, and that's the main reason you're swinging those sticks.

For that matter, even the 19th hole isn't the best place for you to talk business. The clubhouse is where you like to hold court, making sure your playing partners leave with a smile on their face, regardless of how poorly they golfed.

By the way, try to curb your tendency to fish for compliments. You're so personable and stylish that the flattery will come without any subtle influences from you.

Tee Time

Because you need lots of time to prepare yourself both mentally and physically in the morning, don't schedule a tee time too early.

As for the time of year, it doesn't really matter. You can play whether it's hot or cold, rainy or sunny. The only advantage to cooler, wetter conditions is that they give you an opportunity to don more of your fashionable golfwear.

Playing Partners

Birdies

GEMINI: Both of you are easygoing and enjoy the game whether you win or lose. Witty and clever, Gemini makes a good friend on and off the course.

LEO: Although you two have entirely different approaches to the game, you click together, perhaps because you have so much to talk about and laugh about—and bet on.

SAGITTARIUS: Because you and Sagittarius are so social, you get along just fine. You tend to look the other way when Sag does something outrageous, but deep down you find it kind of fun.

AQUARIUS: As air signs, you both accept each other's different golfing styles. You each have something to offer the other: your balance and Aquarius's determination.

Bogeys

LIBRA: If you two are partners, the game could take all day, because you're both so slow and indecisive. Even worse, you two could wage serious head games against each other.

CAPRICORN: Your approach to golf is so different from Capricorn's. This golfer is driven and goal-oriented—something you're not. Beware: You could unwittingly trigger Capricorn's temper.

SCORPIO: This golfer's intensity and competitive nature are mismatched with your easygoing, witty personality. Quite frankly, you don't understand what makes Scorpio tick.

PISCES: Although you share some of the same traits, you can get turned off by Pisces's gamesmanship as well as his or her tendency to ask you very personal questions.

Pars

ARIES: You can have an enjoyable round together, as long as you both share the same cultural background. However, Aries might annoy you by trying to hurry you.

TAURUS: While Taurus tries to be a good partner, the bull can be stubborn and tip your scales. Be careful not to needle this golfer or you could get gored.

CANCER: When conversing on the course, Cancer is often in sync with you and makes a good partner. However, watch out for Cancer's insecurities.

VIRGO: You could learn much from Virgo's sense and sensibility, but most likely you find this golfer a tad too inhibited and quiet.

Glen Day

David Duval

Corey Pavin

Fuzzy Zoeller

Gary Player

Jay Sigel

Dave Stockton

Tom Weiskopf

Rosie Jones

Patty Sheehan

the**scorpio**golfer

passionate

focused

mysterious

intuitive

stoic

(October 24 – November 22)

Y ou like to keep an air of mystery surrounding you, which often keeps others off balance. You are somewhat of a contradiction. You're a passionate person who has strong beliefs and ideas, yet you don't readily share your thoughts and feelings. In fact, you can pretty much keep a poker face. You often appear to have a cool exterior, although underneath you're a boiling cauldron. If people were to watch only your face during a round, they wouldn't know if you had made an eagle or a triple bogey.

▼

Says David Duval, "I always know there are going to be more bad times than good times in this game. So I think you need to enjoy the game, but I don't get overly excited about it. I try to stick with what I do. Either it works or it doesn't. Either I win or I lose."

▲

Staying on an even keel is vital to your success on the golf course. You need to follow your game plan and do the best you can. Some days everything clicks and your shots are as accurate as cruise missiles; other days, you're in the woods so much you need a compass to find your way to the greens. Just hang in there and play one shot at a time.

At the 1991 U.S. Open, Corey Pavin was one shot off the lead before misfiring in the third round for a 7-over 79. "I played lousy the whole day," he recalled. "My game was gone. But I kept my faith up that things were going to get better. I just kept at it. I never got upset. When I finished the round, I knew I had done the best I could—that day. Sometimes your best is 79. But it didn't even faze me. I went out the next day with the same attitude and shot 72 and finished in the top ten."

You know how to work those intense eyes to your advantage. They can be very intimidating. Whoever plays with you better be into the game, because you are a fierce competitor and you expect your playing partners to give it their all. Your intensity either helps the other golfers raise their caliber of play or it causes them to crumble under the pressure.

Pressure is your middle name. You love it because it brings out the best in you. Usually you can handle the stress of a crucial shot or putt only if you stay completely focused. You need to block out all distractions and concentrate totally on that one shot.

You're always trying to improve, no matter how well you shoot.

▼

David Duval became one of only three golfers in PGA history to post a 59 when he came from seven shots back in the final round to win the 1999 Bob Hope Chrysler Classic. "I still have to keep trying to improve, though," he says. "I have lots of goals. I want to get better."

▲

Equipment

Your investigative nature plays a big part in the selection of your equipment. Read everything you can about different kinds of clubs and talk to all the successful golfers you know before making any decision.

If you're just getting into golf, you might rent clubs for a while to be sure you enjoy the game. If you already have that passion, buy a new set. The right balance and size are important to you, but so is your intuitive feeling that these clubs are winners.

You're not likely to own lots of different clubs, but don't hesitate to trade them in for the latest sticks if you have a gut feeling that they are no longer helping you reach your goals.

Attire

You're more likely to dress down than up, to dress for comfort over style. You're there to win and improve your

game, not to make a fashion statement. You have a magnet-
ism that attracts others, so you don't really need trendy
golfwear.

Avoid wearing loud colors and patterns because they're
not really you. Stick with dark, solid colors. Gary Player, for
example, often wears his trademark black shirt, pants, and
cap. However, for most Scorpios maroon is their power color.

If you want to show off a little individuality, do it with
your accessories. Because your strong eyes need protection
anyway, wear a pair of cool or funky sunglasses. Or choose a
hat with an intriguing—and preferably obscure—logo that
leaves your playing partners guessing what it means.

Game Preparation

As a Scorpio, your initial thoughts about your planned
game should start with your previous round. Try to learn
from the past—especially not to repeat the same mistakes. If
you had trouble on the green, take extra time working on
your putting. If you were smacking undesirable hooks during
your last outing, go to the driving range and hit a couple of
buckets' worth of balls.

Senior PGA Tour pro Jay Sigel had one of his worst putting days (thirty-three putts) in the third round of the 1998
EMC Kaanapali Classic in Hawaii. "It was a real shocker,"
he recalled. Sigel was so concerned he took his putter into
his room that Saturday night and worked on his stroke. "I

didn't sleep with it, but I was thinking about it. I practiced a lot in my room and I was up early putting on the green, trying to keep the rhythm." He putted much better the next day, shooting a 68 to win the tournament.

▲

You truly believe that you alone can change bad habits and patterns. However, you could save time by seeking expert help. A good pro can help you resolve playing problems. Your tendency, as you know, is to assume that you can do it better yourself. If that means changing clubs, balls, or partners, you're prepared to do it.

Once you psych yourself up, you're ready to play. While not one to boast, you'll let others in your foursome know that you feel great and are planning to break your handicap. The statement is less an actual fact and more a way to pump yourself up. It's also meant as a veiled challenge to the others to play their very best.

Your Game

Off the Tee

As you step into the tee box, empty all thoughts from your mind and let your subconscious take over. The less thinking here, the better.

Take several practice swings until your intuition tells you the time is right to address the ball. It's okay to waggle and adjust your feet, because you need to release some of your pent-up energy.

An easy takeaway, a smooth swing, and a natural follow-through will happen if you don't clutter your mind. For your size, you probably have a strong drive. But Scorpios are prone to hooks and slices. If you launched an errant tee shot, remember to keep your cool. A temper tantrum at the tee box undoubtedly will carry over onto the fairway and could ruin your day.

On the Fairway

You're not afraid to take calculated chances, especially on your approaches. You trust your irons, which is good, but sometimes your overconfidence can hurt you more than help you.

Consider the options and then go with your instincts. Accept the fact that sometimes you'll be dead-on and sometimes you'll be way off. Be mindful that you have a tendency to use too much club because you have a strong swing powered by that tightly wound intensity inside you.

If airmailing the green is a chronic problem, take time at the practice tee to recalibrate your irons. But instead of being relaxed when you practice, try to get into the same intense frame of mind you have during a real game. Then you'll get a true picture of your irons' yardage.

In the Hazard

For the typical Scorpio, success or failure pretty much relies on how you approach the problem. If you're seething inside because you got into this mess, you'll only make matters worse. If you view the situation as a challenge that you feel you can overcome, you have a much better chance of getting up and down.

The key is to maintain your composure and not let bunkers, sand, or water deter you from playing your game.

On the Green

The most important rule for you, Scorpio, is *relax*. Because you're such an intense player, you need to find a way to relieve the tension when you reach the green.

▼

Says Fuzzy Zoeller, "I don't concentrate when I'm walking down the fairway [toward the green]. You have to give yourself a little break and then get back into it [focusing]. So I do anything I can to relax. I whistle or talk to my playing partners. I try to focus only when I pull the putter out of my bag."

▲

Course Management

It's all about rhythm and following through on your strategy. You need to maintain a pace that's right for you: not so fast that you're making quick decisions; not so slow that you become indecisive.

Until 1998, Glen Day was nicknamed "All Day" by his fellow golfers because he was considered the slowest player on the tour. When he learned how to simplify the process of hitting a golf ball and play at a faster (but not fast) pace, he finished fifteenth on the PGA money list in 1998. "The reason I get so slow is I try to go through a thinking process," he said, "but I believe I play better if I make up my mind and hit it."

Says fellow competitor Fred Funk, "David Duval gets in this rhythm and he never gets out of it. He never hits a shot until he's ready to hit it, never hits a putt until he feels comfortable."

Don't let your temper get the best of you, because it will cloud your judgment and cause you to lose your focus. Just ask Tom Weiskopf or Patty Sheehan. Many times they encountered disasters in major tournaments after they lost their cool.

Corey Pavin's temper often jarred him enough to cause him to lose his focus. Several times, after bad tee shots, he smashed his driver against the tee markers so hard it exploded like a bomb. But then he developed an improved mental approach. The next year, 1991, Pavin soared to the top of the money list.

Wagering

You're a daring player and an even more daring gambler. You love a good wager, especially a push, because it adds pressure and helps you stay focused. You have an all-or-nothing approach and like to play double or nothing if someone is willing. But just as you can win big, you also can lose big. Think carefully about who you are playing before getting into these big wagers.

You're not into gamesmanship, and you expect others not to attempt mind games. If they do, stay cool. The slightest crack in your stoic demeanor could spell trouble for you. Rely on your ability to stay focused or you'll be heading to the ATM machine after your round.

Let's Talk

You enjoy pleasant conversation as long as it's not about yourself. You'd rather people didn't know too much about you. After all, you want to maintain a certain air of mystery.

You're quite personable because you know how to draw others—no matter how shy they are—into an interesting dialogue. Be careful that the questions you ask—and you do ask a lot—aren't too probing or personal. You can be manipulative, and if you want to find out something about someone, you usually manage to do so.

You also have a bad habit of putting your foot in your mouth. No matter what your intentions, you tend to say something that ticks off a playing partner, causing you to spend a lot of time apologizing.

Fuzzy Zoeller, one of the PGA Tour's most popular personalities, found himself in hot water after the 1997 Masters when he was talking to a camera crew about Tiger Woods's record-shattering win: "You pat him on the back and say, 'Congratulations' and 'Enjoy it' and tell him not to serve fried chicken next year [at the Masters champions dinner] . . . or collard greens. Or whatever the hell they serve."

Faced with charges that his comments were racially charged, Zoeller denied any ill intent. "I meant it as a joke. If I offended anybody by what I said, I apologize on the spot. I didn't think anything of it. I'm a jokester."

For weeks after, Zoeller was lambasted by the press and various African-American groups. His main sponsor, Kmart, dropped him. Eventually, Zoeller apologized in person to Tiger, who accepted his apology.

Because you're so focused while playing golf, it's wise if you don't discuss business on the course. Keep the conversation light during the round and save the important stuff for the 19th hole.

Tee Time

You tend to play best in early mornings and late afternoons.

You should avoid strong sun whenever possible. Cloudy days can be good for you because you really don't like intense light or heat. Your top performances on the course are likely to occur in the fall and spring. The cool weather and lower sun make for excellent times to play.

Playing Partner

Birdies

CANCER: This golfer can be a competitive playing part-ner for you. Not only that, but Cancer just might offer you a few tips that could prove quite helpful.

VIRGO: You both are impressed with the other's balanced, disciplined approach to the game. You're not likely to talk a lot to each other, but you have an unspoken bond.

CAPRICORN: You two get along well because you like to talk about mutual interests. You both have similar ambitions and share the same belief that you create your own destiny.

PISCES: You're both water signs and have an intuitive sense about each other. If anyone can best understand what's underneath that cool exterior of yours, it's Pisces.

Bogeys

LEO: This golfer has a strong personality that can rub you the wrong way. Don't get into any debates or drop any snide remarks. It's best to let your clubs do the talking.

LIBRA: This golfer's easygoing, witty personality are mis-matched with your intense, competitive nature. Quite frankly, you just don't understand what makes Libra tick.

SAGITTARIUS: This golfer's fun-loving, energetic ways don't cut it with you. Unintentionally, Sag can quickly get on your nerves, causing you to say something that you'll quickly regret.

AQUARIUS: Your emotional thermostats are set at opposite ends of the dial. Trying to figure each other out is about as easy as draining a fifty-foot downhill putt.

Pars

ARIES: You can identify with Aries' competitive nature and have a spirited game, but be careful because one of you is liable to say or do something that will ignite the other's temper.

TAURUS: Although your intensity and competitiveness are traits that tend to clash with this easygoing golfer, Taurus can help you stay focused and balanced.

GEMINI: Both you and Gemini are fairly intuitive golfers who get along fine even though your personalities are so different. Keep cool if Gemini pulls a joke on you.

SCORPIO: You can respect another Scorpio, but being the same sign can create some fairway drama. If you both stay focused on golf, the game can be enjoyable.

Steve Elkington

Jay Haas

Scott Hoch

Tom Kite

Rocco Mediate

Constantino Rocca

Paul Stankowski

Lanny Wadkins

Joe Inman

Lee Trevino

Danielle Ammaccapane

Tammie Green

Lorie Kane

Barb Mucha

Karrie Webb

the**sagittarius**golfer

extroverted

optimistic

energetic

fun-loving

daring

(November 23 — December 21)

A fire sign, Sagittarius is the extrovert of the golf course. Ruled by Jupiter, you like things big—big expectations in life and on the course.

Of all the signs, you're most likely to try to improve your golf game through new-age methods, including meditation and yoga. And because you generally are superstitious, you may even carry a good-luck charm.

▼

At the 1997 Sprint Titleholders Championship, Tammie Green finished the third round with a ten-footer for birdie. But when she arrived at her hotel, she realized she had left her lucky coin behind at the 18th green. Tammie was worried that the dime, with which she had marked the ball, would be stolen or washed away. When she returned early the next day, she looked for the dime and found it. She wound up winning the tourney.

▲

Most importantly, though, you're the ultimate optimist. Even if you're down by ten strokes and there are only three holes left to play, you still think there's a chance to win. That's because you truly believe you've plugged into the power of luck, Zen, positive thinking, or all three. You live in the here and now, not the past. You accept with a sense of predestination that whatever happens is supposed to happen, so you don't get too uptight over wayward shots.

This unique belief system gives you the courage to seem fearless on the course. Nothing can stop you from attempting an otherwise white-knuckle, knee-knocking, sphincter-tightening shot. If you make it, terrific. If not, hey, it wasn't meant to be. Fear will never sneak into your golf bag.

Barb Mucha, winner of the 1998 Sara Lee Classic, said, "A friend once told me, 'Don't let the fear of failure be greater than your desire to succeed.' Doubt can creep in, but I don't want fear motivating me."

Tom Kite accepts his bad shots, shrugs them off, and concentrates completely on the next one. As he puts it, "Golf is not a game of perfect."

This doesn't mean you don't try to eliminate your golfing mistakes. But you understand that while it's important to strive for perfection, it's detrimental to demand perfection from yourself. On the other hand, seeking enjoyment on the links is a top priority.

To you, the golf course is a place to have fun—lots of fun—by displaying not only your shot-making skills but your wise-cracking humor as well.

▼

Lee Trevino has become a legend as golf's guru of guffaws. On his ball striking: "I'm not saying my golf game went bad, but if I grew tomatoes, they'd come up sliced." After he was struck by lightning: "'Damn,' I thought to myself, 'this is a helluva penalty for slow play.'"

Steve Elkington can tell jokes that would make anyone blush—although he's smart enough to make sure no one is tape-recording or filming him when he gets to the punch line.

▲

Golf Equipment

While it's always hard to generalize physical characteristics, Sagittarians come closest to showing some similarity in their physical makeup. There are two prominent aspects of their physique: a disproportionately long torso or long, lanky limbs. This makes them need extra care in selecting clubs. You should get professional assistance if you fall into the above category. If you take the game seriously, you should have custom clubs made to fit your unique body.

Don't ever think you must crouch or choke up on the clubs for a comfortable fit. Also, don't buy a set of used clubs because they probably won't fit you very well.

You have excellent stamina and energy, but you aren't necessarily the strongest sign of the zodiac. You'll probably do best with graphite shafts that have a good flex.

A note of caution, however. If you're a typical Sagittarius, you can be gullible, so get references before you choose a good club fitter. Don't spend more than you need for good clubs, and be wary of getting talked into buying unnecessary golf gadgets and gimmicks.

Attire

The best way to describe your golf attire is sporty. Not conservative and not flashy, you usually find the latest styles in golfwear. Whatever you choose, it'll look good on you because you know how to carry yourself. You're not a sloucher, and you always walk with your head held high.

Deep, rich colors help channel your energy and provide you with an uplifting mystical force. For you, the best colors are purple, lavender, turquoise, royal blue, and magenta.

You don't like synthetic clothes, so wear cottons and natural fabrics. If you want to make a political or personal statement, wear a hat or visor that touts your latest cause or your current philosophy.

Game Preparation

Every time you go out to play golf, you have great expectations that this round will be the best you've ever played. To you, the game is fun, and you look forward to a stress-free four hours.

You're probably the least likely of all the signs to want to spend much time at the practice tee or green before your round. You just aren't into practicing.

Nevertheless, there are plenty of things you should do to prepare. First, spend a few minutes getting yourself in the right frame of mind through guided imagery or transcendental meditation or whatever technique it takes to get you completely relaxed.

Next, hit some balls at the range while visualizing how you will play the course. Then, go to the practice green and focus on your putting. It's imperative that you don't just go through the motions. Try your best to sink each putt.

Finally, set a realistic goal for yourself. Talk to yourself. Get in touch with your inner core and make a pact between your heart, soul, and mind that you will do everything you can to achieve that goal.

Your Game

Off the Tee

The tee box always gets your blood flowing. It's probably because you feel it's the best place for you to unleash all that energy flowing through your body.

But be careful. You can get so wound up trying to kill the ball that you do nothing more than top a weenie dribbler that barely makes it past the tee markers.

Relax, take some deep breaths, and loosen the death grip you have on the club. After a slow takeaway, direct your energy on the downswing. Remember, stay calm.

If you whack a liner that sends the birds and squirrels fleeing for their lives, watch your mouth. You have a tendency to let loose with words that could make a drill sergeant blush.

On the Fairway

Your iron work tends to be the weakest part of your game. Most often it's not from a lack of mechanics but from a lack of smarts. Sagittarians have a habit of making bad decisions on the fairway—going for the water-fronted green even though you don't have enough club or airmailing the green because you didn't take the tailwind into account.

Play smart, play wisely. Plan your shot before you get to the ball and pay attention to the conditions. Destiny won't get you a par nearly as often as your brains will.

In the Hazard

If you're a typical Sagittarius, it shouldn't matter how many times you've wound up in the drink or the sand. Forget about it. You live in the present, not the past. Focus on the next shot only, not how you got there and certainly not how you blew it the last time you wound up in the same hazard.

In 1989, at the Nestlé Invitational, Tom Kite and Davis Love III were locked in a play-off. Kite hit his approach in the water. He then had to play a long wedge shot over the same water to a tight pin. He could have dwelled on the way he hit the last shot badly. He could have tried for the middle of the green or even the bunker, just to make sure he didn't make two splashes in a row. Instead, he hit that second wedge stiff, made the putt, and went on to win.

▲

One more thing: Sagittarians have a tendency to be clumsy. Look out for the rake in the sand, the tree roots in the rough, the mud by the pond. If anyone trips, stumbles, or falls, it'll likely be you.

On the Green

You have an excellent putting eye. Put less thought into the mechanics of your putting stroke and more into reading the green. Once you've determined your line, get settled and putt the ball. Don't waste time. The longer you linger over a putt, the worse it will get.

Even if your game up to that point hasn't been good, your optimism will make sure you have few three-putts. Besides, you're always good for one or two lucky breaks on the green.

On the negative side: The green is the most likely place for you to utter a remark that, no matter how unintentional, is just too blunt or too hurtful for your playing partners to laugh off.

Course Management

You definitely need to play a fast game. If your partners are turtles, you'll get so frustrated you'll subconsciously be hitting shots in the rough just to use up the extra energy it takes to find the ball and plan your recovery.

Don't worry if you start off a little rocky. You have an almost unlimited supply of energy and optimism—and if you have a short-term memory loss, you'll straighten yourself out. You'll be just as strong by the 18th hole as you were on the first tee.

You need to play a smart but fearless style if you ever want to improve. If you don't think you have the grit to nail that must-make shot, look deep within yourself, because it's there.

▼

On the 18th hole on the final day of the 1983 Ryder Cup, Lanny Wadkins was one down to José Maria Canizáres, with the U.S. tied with Europe. Wadkins faced a third shot of eighty yards to a pin cut hard against the edge of a watery peninsula. Anything more than a birdie and the U.S. would fail to win the Cup for the first time in twenty-six years. Wadkins stepped up in his brisk way and buzzed a low-flying shot directly at the flag. The ball spun to a stop eighteen inches from the hole, earning the most precious halve the Ryder Cup had ever seen. The shot was so instantly legendary that moments later, after the U.S. had won 14 ½ to 13 ½, Jack Nicklaus kissed the divot made by Wadkins's sand wedge.

▲

Wagering

Boy, do you love to gamble. It adds excitement to the game and ratchets up the pressure, which tends to make you a better player.

Amid all the backslapping and congratulations that Wadkins received after his gutsy approach at the 1983 Ryder Cup, he opened his mouth only to find he couldn't speak. "That was the most pressure I have ever felt over a shot," Wadkins recalled. "But feeling pressure means you are where you want to be. That's when it's fun. That's when it means something."

▲

Whether you have the bucks to lose or not, you can sometimes get carried away with your big bets. But you need to watch your wagering because you can lose big. Like it or not, you can't win on only hope or luck, even though at times you think you can. And if others don't want to bet as much as you, don't become overbearing or you'll turn off your playing partners before you even reach the first tee.

Unless you're teaming up with an Aries, a Leo or another Sag, avoid team wagers. You like to rely on your own skills when there's money on the line.

Let's Talk

You're a fun, cheerful, expressive person who is generally loved by all. People gather around you because of your
marvelous, energetic personality—and your jokes.

Because you're a natural salesperson, you can sell just
about anything. But try not to talk business on the course.
Use the time to reveal yourself as the kind, likable, dependable person you really are. Letting others see you this way is
an important aspect of any relationship, business or otherwise.

Save business talk for later. Quite frankly, though, even at
the 19th hole you'd probably much rather talk about your
most recent causes or philosophical ideas.

Tee Time

When it comes to tee times, you can be ready to play
anytime from early morning to early evening. It doesn't matter because your energy level is high from the moment you
wake up in the morning (which typically is quite early).

You do, however, believe in luck, and you might have a
lucky day of the week that you'd rather play on if possible.

Although you're adaptable to most any time of the year
or to any weather conditions, you tend to golf your best in
warm weather. Sagittarians like Steve Elkington seem to play
better golf in late summer.

Playing Partners

Birdies

ARIES: You both play fast and hard, leaving the rest in the rough. Aries's spirited energy matches yours, making for a fun, active time on the course.

LEO: This golfer's enthusiasm and ambition to win appeal to you in a big way. Your occasional frank remark may ruffle Leo's mane, but it won't spoil the relationship.

LIBRA: You really appreciate Libra's wit and charm and can have a fun time on the course. You love nothing better than making a bet with Libra—and winning.

SAGITTARIUS: You two could shoot triple figures and still have a super time. The game can almost become incidental if you two are cracking jokes and sharing new-age insights.

Bogeys

TAURUS: Taurus is just too slow and plodding for you and offers no real excitement. This golfer just doesn't appreciate your impulsive, fun-loving behavior on the course.

CANCER: This golfer often finds your antics just too distracting. An offhand comment about Cancer or a joke at Cancer's expense can leave you with a hurt or sullen partner.

VIRGO: Off the course you and Virgo share similar causes, but this golfer is too slow and deliberate for you. Besides, Virgo doesn't get your jokes.

SCORPIO: Unintentionally, you can quickly get on Scorpio's nerves, causing Scorpio to thoughtlessly say something that could take the fun out of your game.

Pars

GEMINI: Both of you are party animals, and when you get together golf may take a back seat to having a good time. Just be careful not to get into a big-money bet or else the fun could vanish.

CAPRICORN: You don't have much in common and your golf philosophies are so different. But you can learn from Capricorn's cautious style, and Capricorn can benefit from your optimism.

AQUARIUS: You can enjoy the fun-loving Aquarius during a round of golf. Neither of you want deep conversations—just a good time. Don't force Aquarius into big bets.

PISCES: You both are adaptable as can be, and your golf relationship should be good, assuming you don't try to tell this golfer how to play.

Paul Azinger

Ben Crenshaw

Steve Jones

Mark O'Meara

Tiger Woods

Hubert Green

Graham Marsh

Leonard Thompson

Brandie Burton

Nancy Lopez

Michelle McGann

Jan Stephenson

the**capricorn**golfer

self-disciplined

goal-oriented

persistent

patient

dependable

(December 22 – January 20)

Unless you're absolutely in love with golf, chances are you don't play very well. However, if you love the smell of freshly cut grass, the sound of an iron thwacking against Surlyn, and the sight of a ball rolling into a cup, then you play this game with gusto.

Every day on the course is a day with a new challenge to face, a goal to achieve. You can't stand mediocrity, either by others or yourself. Nothing you do is halfway: It's all or nothing. You know to be good at golf will take dedication and patience. Fortunately, you have both. Should you decide to pursue the game to its fullest, you'll be one of the best. There is an irony in those ruled by the planet Saturn: You have to be the best because you are so often plagued by self-doubt and low self-esteem.

▼

In 1995, after a winless streak of over two years, Nancy Lopez wondered if she would ever finish first again and questioned her desire to play on the tour. "I resigned myself to either get more prepared and get in shape or quit playing golf," Nancy recalled.

For the next two years, she sweated on a Stairmaster, pounded range balls in between PTA meetings, and lost forty pounds while taking care of her three children. The hard work and self-discipline paid off. Her game got better, and she won the 1997 Chick-fil-A Charity Championship.

You are driven by a need to set goals and then do whatever it takes to reach them. This is a trait that you carry from your everyday life to the golf course.

Steve Jones suffered a near career-ending dirt-bike accident in 1991. But he made it his goal to return to the PGA Tour. It took him four years to do it. Then he made it a goal to win a major. A year later, he won the 1996 U.S. Open.

In 1993, Paul Azinger was one of the best golfers on the tour. However, just months after winning the PGA Championship, he was diagnosed with lymphoma. But he refused to wallow in self-pity. He set goals and went after them. He finished fifth in the 1998 Masters, only three shots behind the winner. "I actually saw myself winning here," he told reporters. "I didn't, and I'm disappointed. But I'm also happy that I'm disappointed." To him, that meant his confidence and determination were returning to their old form.

▲

Like Tiger Woods, you can unleash an angry outburst. You can cuss at your Titleist, glare contemptuously at putts that don't fall, and helicopter a wedge into the pond.

You can appear somewhat menacing, a squinting grimace sweeping across your face as you follow the flight of your ball. But then you'll make a goofy gesture, toss off a carefree quip, and flash a smile that will make your playing partners smile back.

Equipment

Because you're very money-conscious and frugal to a fault at times, don't choose expensive clubs or accessories. You might try to rent clubs for a while until you decide to take the game seriously. Then you should spend good money for a high-quality set.

Although you always like to be in control, get some help from a pro in making your selection. This pro, by the way, could ultimately be your golfing mentor. You're known to seek out mentors in all your pursuits.

Whatever clubs, bag, and accessories you buy, you'll probably keep them your whole golf lifetime—and pass them down to your kids because, well, you're a Capricorn.

▼

Through slumps and victories, injuries and good health, Steve Jones's center-shafted Bullseye with the green overwrap on the grip has been his constant companion since his rookie year in 1982. "I ought to bronze that thing when I'm done with my career," said Jones, who needed only ninety-nine putts in his victory at the 1997 Phoenix Open.

Attire

You won't skimp here, and the reason is simple. You always dress for success, whether it's on the golf course or at the office. You believe that people look at you and determine your success by what you wear. Your selection of golf clothes goes to the high-end brand names. A typical Capricorn doesn't blindly dress in the latest fads, but that's only because quality is first and foremost.

Your power colors are dark blue and indigo.

Accessories play a big role in your golfwear. Whether you're a man or woman, you tend to wear jewelry on the course. Hats, caps, and visors also are a big deal with you, and you have a closet full of them.

▼

Of course, no Capricorn is as hat-obsessed as Michelle McGann. She has hundreds of hats. She also has more than sixty pairs of FootJoy shoes color-coordinated to blend with her outfits. Dozens of baseball caps designed by Taylor Made match her own line of clothes.

Says fellow Capricorn Nancy Lopez, "I think her hats

and her jewelry and the way she appears on the golf course are wonderful. It's great for our tour to have somebody who has a sparkling taste in clothes."

▲

Game Preparation

If you're serious about playing well, you need to develop a pregame practice routine that includes specific goals for the day.

Just as your sign is symbolized by the goat scaling the mountain, you should see each game as climbing toward a goal. Usually all you want is to better your score from the previous round, or to stay out of the rough, or to two-putt every green. It could also be that you want to beat a playing partner or firm up that business commitment.

During the week prior to the game, head to the practice range and work on improving one particular part of your game. You might end up spending hours there in a determined quest to see the improvement you've been seeking. Just don't get too frustrated if it's slow in coming.

▼

One time, Mark O'Meara was practicing in a bone-chilling rain and refused to leave. "We were trying to make my backswing better and I just couldn't get it right," he recalled. Frustrated, O'Meara started throwing clubs. Eventually, all he had left was his bag and umbrella. He quit only after his swing coach told him, "Sorry, Mark, I can't give you a lesson with an umbrella."

▲

Your Game

Off the Tee

Your drives are controlled by the level of nervousness you process. You know everybody is watching, and your biggest fear in life is to be humiliated. Should you top the ball or hit it poorly, the embarrassment will haunt you the rest of the game. Therefore, pure concentration on the swing and follow-through is most important. You've practiced enough, so you know what works well. If you do screw up, it's usually because of a poor follow-through. You tend to look up too quickly and see how your playing partners reacted to your shot. Others really don't care that much and are more interested in their own game. Once you acquire the confidence of the Capricorn pros, you'll improve your handicap tremendously.

On the Fairway

If your short game is long on shanks and slices, you need to take a step back and be a little more analytical rather than critical. You can get down on yourself very quickly, and that will cause you to get reckless, especially on your approaches. You normally aren't considered a risk taker. Be deliberate and be careful not to play too fast on your approach shots. Keep in mind all that you learned from your pro about using your irons, and you'll reap great rewards.

In the Hazard

After you get over your anger at landing in a hazard, you tend to get the ball out of this situation as quickly as possible. Take your time. Try to lighten up and call on your dry sense of humor to ease your frustration.

Then use your analytical skills and view your escape shot as a challenge. If you want to attempt a risky shot, this is the place to do it. Just don't get too upset if it doesn't work out the way you want. Keep plugging away, and you'll eventually find routine success in hitting safely out of the bunkers.

On the Green

You're an excellent putter who has a good eye and can size up a putt quickly. Be careful not to second-guess yourself. Although you're somewhat of an analytical player, you should putt more by feel and gut.

▼

Tiger Woods' putting woes in 1998 were traced to a change in technique, his father Earl told reporters at the time. "The general problem is that he got away from his basic style of putting. He is an instinctive type of putter. He has gotten too concerned with mechanics and is thinking too much about hand pressure and all sorts of things instead of trusting his stroke."

▲

Watch out for your temper. If it's going to explode, it likely will happen on the green. If you blow an easy putt, your anger and embarrassment could send you into bogeyland.

However, you're very particular about golf etiquette, and it shows on the green. You're quiet and respectful of others and know when and how to mark your ball. You expect others to do the same.

Course Management

You tend to play consistent, but not flashy, golf. That's fine because that's your style and you should stick with it. Be deliberate and plan each shot. Keep your short-term goals in mind whenever you get the urge to do something wild and crazy on the course, like thinking you can get the ball out from behind that tree by choking up on your three-iron and bouncing the ball off the rock wall and onto the fairway.

Play it safe. Sure, it's not thrilling and exciting and you won't get the oohs and aahs from your playing partners. But what you probably will get are the bucks from your pals for winning the round's bets.

Guard against getting too uptight in difficult situations. Usually you perform quite well under pressure as long as you don't get too tense. You need to keep focusing on your goals for the round. Remember, you are in control of your own fate.

Mark O'Meara won the 1998 Masters with a birdie putt on the final hole. "I told myself, 'Am I nervous? Yeah, but there's no need to go to a play-off. I've got it in my hands and I can finish it off.'"

▲

Wagering

You're not much of a gambler. You believe in hard work and long hours to achieve positive results. You're quite frugal and don't like throwing away money on foolish things such as gambling.

However, you don't want to be a wet blanket, so go along with others in whatever betting game they choose. If you're playing well, pick and choose the holes in which you want to press.

You do better on individual wagers than team wagers because you don't like to depend on others for your success. Actually, a bet with someone who plays at your level could be quite beneficial for you. It will help you bear down more and make that extra little effort that could spell the difference between a birdie and a par.

▼

Fellow Capricorns Tiger Woods and Mark O'Meara have become best friends—the young, single, black multi-millionaire and the middle-aged, portfolio-nurturing, balding white father of two. They each learn from the other. "There are things I can learn from Tiger, especially his tremendous drive," said O'Meara.

They also push each other when they play fun rounds for $50 or $100. Says Johnny Miller, "O'Meara is a competitive guy, and playing all those goof-off games against Tiger at Isleworth [near Orlando] made him improve. He just wouldn't give in to Tiger and it completely changed his outlook. I guarantee you, if O'Meara didn't live near Tiger, he wouldn't have won a major." O'Meara won both the Masters and the British Open in 1998.

You have a lot of integrity and wouldn't do anything to take advantage of others by playing any kind of head games with your playing partners. You also won't cut others any slack if they want a mulligan or seek some sort of relief because you're a stickler for the rules.

Let's Talk

You're ready anytime to talk about what you like most— your work and the stock market. Even if it's not to make a deal, you'll discuss business every chance you get on the course. In fact, you don't have much else to talk about.

But you are a social being and want to be liked, so join in any conversation. If you don't like the subject, use that subtle skill of yours to change it.

Tee Time

Because of your cool disposition, you play best at cool

times of the day. You especially like early mornings, since you always have a full day planned. Rarely do you play during the week, because that would take you away from work.

It really makes no difference to you what time of the year it is, as long as it's not too hot. Cold, rainy weather doesn't affect you nearly as much as hot, steamy weather does.

Playing Partners

Birdies

TAURUS: You both play a disciplined, consistent golf. Taurus has the temperament, willingness, and analytical mind to be an excellent mentor for you.

VIRGO: You and Virgo tend to share the same values in golf and in life. Because Virgo is so good at analyzing shots, he or she can also be a good mentor for you.

SCORPIO: You like talking to each other about business and other mutual interests. You both believe you create your own destiny, and you have similar ambitions on and off the course.

CAPRICORN: A pairing linked by mutual respect, you both understand the importance of hard work, discipline, and setting goals. If you two can lighten up, you'll have a lot of fun.

Bogeys

GEMINI: This golfer is just a little too wild for you. Gemini's free spirit and joking ways can drive you to distraction or ignite your temper.

LIBRA: Your approach to golf is so different from Libra's. This golfer is just too easygoing for your tastes. Besides, Libra has the ability to unwittingly get under your skin.

AQUARIUS: You find Aquarius's unconventional method of play appalling at times. This is a golfer who can say and do things on and off the course that leave you shaking your head in disbelief.

PISCES: You two aren't compatible. In your eyes, Pisces isn't competitive enough and is much too sensitive. You can't tolerate this golfer's gamesmanship either.

Pars

ARIES: You both play the game with intensity and enjoy the competition. But be careful, because you both know how to trigger each other's volatile temper.

CANCER: You two can be quite compatible, as long as you watch what you say. You can be so driven that you could exploit many of Cancer's insecurities.

LEO: Like you, Leo enjoys the best of everything, so you tend to appreciate each other. Leo's intensity and enthusiasm can either encourage you or overwhelm you.

SAGITTARIUS: Even though you don't have much in common and your golf philosophy is so different, playing a round with Sag could put a smile on your face.

Billy Andrade

Bob Estes

Jack Nicklaus

Greg Norman

José Maria Olazábal

Nick Price

Payne Stewart

Curtis Strange

José Maria Canizáres

Bob Dickson

Bob Murphy

Bruce Summerhays

Jane Geddes

Patty Berg

Carol Mann

Mickey Wright

the**aquarius**golfer

complex

analytical

inventive

eccentric

personable

(January 21 — February 19)

Ruled by the planet Uranus, Aquarians are the
most contradictory golfers of the zodiac. In addition to the
free will of Uranus, you are influenced by the conservative
nature of Saturn. With this unusual combination, it's just
about impossible to tie you down to anything.

You're an engaging individual who's well liked by just
about everyone. You're a joiner of many groups and probably
have played in more charity events than any of your non-
Aquarian friends. However, you shy away from those close
one-on-one relationships even on the golf course.

While golf is a game primarily of mechanics, you're a
person of theory. But if you have the mechanics, you sometimes pay less attention to golf theory, much to your detri-
ment. You certainly are inventive and have your own ways of
attacking the course.

Some of the world's greatest golfers are Aquarians.
This is due to their great attitude, innovative nature, and ability to relax even in a throat-tightening situation. There's also
a certain air about them that sets them apart from the rest.
Greg Norman always has that swagger, that I'm-better-than-
you attitude. Jack Nicklaus invented it. Curtis Strange

acquired it. Meanwhile, Payne Stewart exuded a bon vivant flair, while Nick Price coolly hides the inner peace to win.

Like the pros, you tend to have a bulldog determination that refuses to let you give up. You will try just as hard no matter the score, the weather, or your health. Quitting is not part of your world.

▼

During the third round of the 1998 U.S. Senior Open, Jack Nicklaus was hobbled by a seriously deteriorating hip and recorded a 79—his highest round ever—to fall out of contention. Many golfers would have lost their motivation. Not the Golden Bear. He shot a blistering 67 in the final round.

▲

Because you're filled with contradictions, you tend to have either too much confidence or sometimes not enough. If you take the long view—beating your opponents or breaking 80—you might get overconfident. If you take the short view—getting up and down from the bunker on the difficult hole you're facing—you could be fighting nerves.

▼

Nick Price learned a hard lesson about overconfidence at the 1982 British Open. He had a three-stroke lead at the 13th tee in the final round. "Well, we've got it now," he boldly told his caddie. But Price bogeyed the 13th, double-bogeyed the 15th, and finished with a 73—one stroke behind winner Tom Watson. "Maybe that experience was a blessing," Price said years later. "Maybe if I'd won, I would've thought, 'Hey, that's all the game I need.'"

In the mid-1980s, Payne Stewart had a tendency to fritter away leads late in the final round because of a lack of confidence. "It was just an inability to deal with the situations," he admitted. "I was scared to hit the shot that could win it all because it might be the one that loses it all."

▲

To avoid these swings of confidence, the top Aquarian golfers stay focused on each shot and don't get ahead of themselves.

Equipment

If it's new and you can afford it, you've got to have it. You're a lover of the latest anything. You're likely to order a new driver or putter from the Golf Channel late at night because you've been convinced that this is the hottest club in the game. And when you whip it out of your bag, you hope others will comment on your new acquisition.

Being of a scientific mind, you probably should choose your clubs using the latest computer techniques. Whatever you select, don't let it be a haphazard decision; make it one thoroughly researched. You should go to the best pros available for advice. Don't bother visiting the sporting goods section of the local department store for your clubs. They're not for you.

Your choice of balls and other accessories should go through the same rigorous routine because you get enjoyment out of the research. However, you should curb your tendency to acquire too many clubs. You're better off finding the right brand and sticking to it for all your clubs. This will help you with consistency, which is not one of your strongest attributes.

You want to be unique, and you're likely to choose a golf bag that's radically different in color and style from anyone else's at the golf course.

Attire

If you had your way, you'd dress for golf depending on whatever way you felt when you woke up that day—maybe an Eagles T-shirt and cutoffs or a purple tank top and red shorts. But you're a stickler for following the rules, and you wouldn't think of violating the course dress codes.

The best colors for you to golf in are royal blue and azure.

You're somewhat of an individualist, so you need to find a way to show off your freshness. Many Aquarians like to wear funny golf caps or hats from the top courses in the world. Others sport odd-looking sunglasses.

▼

When it comes to fashion, few Aquarians would go to the extreme that Payne Stewart did. His colorful cap-and-knickers ensemble made him one of the most instantly recognized personalities on the golf course. The most famous wardrobe in golf was born at the 1982 Atlanta Classic when Stewart noticed six players dressed exactly as he was—in red slacks, white shirt, and white shoes. "I vowed right then I wasn't going to be another look-alike golfer," said Stewart, who had a twenty-foot-long closet that was barely big enough to hold all his knickers.

▲

Game Preparation

Since Aquarius is ruled by both Saturn and Uranus, how you prepare for the game will depend on which of the two has a stronger influence.

If it's Saturn, you'll take a more traditional approach. You'll get to the course early and spend equal amounts of time on the practice tee and the putting green. You'll do all these things methodically and create a feeling of security before teeing off.

If, on the other hand, you have Uranus as the dominant influence, your game preparation could change drastically from week to week. You might hit a few balls and then spend the rest of the time psyching yourself up. Or you might show up late, do a few stretching exercises, and then go right to the first tee—but after first checking your astrological forecast for the day.

The best Aquarian golfers manage to strike a balance between physical and mental preparation to find success on the course.

Your Game

Off the Tee

You're a great analyzer, so put your analytical mind to work at the tee box. If possible, wait until the others have teed off so you can study the wind and course conditions.

Your drives are usually well executed, partly because you focus more on your woods than your irons, and partly because you have the newest, most advanced driver in the foursome.

Here's a tip that works well with Aquarians: Check your swing at home in front of a mirror—without a golf ball, of course. You'll learn a lot about your swing. The images that are created in front of the mirror transfer well to swing images in your mind during actual play. (Besides, you like to look at yourself.)

On the Fairway

Aquarians tend to be big hitters. Here's where you can follow the lead of Jack Nicklaus: Learn to use restraint. In his prime, the Golden Bear knew that, based on his temperament, he needed to play conservatively most of the time. He used his length intelligently, like an expert fly fisherman letting out line and pulling it back in. He was aggressive on the par-5's but shot mostly for the middle of the greens on the other holes. He made sure he never beat himself.

In the Hazard

As bad as hazards are, they can provide you with an opportunity to be your most inventive. Using that great mind of yours, find a way to weasel out of the tightest spots. You're not a reckless golfer and you don't take unnecessary chances, but do whatever it takes to get up and down.

It's vital that you let the analytical side of you block out any creeping thoughts of pressure or self-doubt.

To ward off pressure, Payne Stewart used a preshot routine every time he was about to address the ball. Such repetition helped give Stewart security. He realized that in a tournament his first drive on Thursday was just as important as Sunday's last putt. That way, Stewart didn't feel more pressure on one shot than on another.

Admits Curtis Strange: "I'm as nervous as anyone else, and I have as much anxiety. But the key is, I enjoy the feeling and I can still concentrate. Nothing makes me feel better than to hit a clutch shot."

▲

On the Green

There's no need to rush. Take the time to study the green and your line by engaging your analytical mind. Once you discover what it takes to sink that putt, clear your head and stroke the ball.

You have a tendency to hit your putts hard, which isn't all that bad because you drain more than your share of putts. However, you also face more than your share of five- to ten-foot comebackers. But in true Aquarian fashion, those putts won't intimidate you.

Course Management

Some Aquarians have a problem with consistency. If you fall into this category, your course management needs to be a little on the conservative side. Remember, your top priority should be to hit the ball straight rather than to hit it long. It's okay to lay up. Better to make par than to take chances and end up with a bogey.

Here's a do and a don't: Do stay focused for each shot. Don't beat yourself up if you mis-hit it.

Nick Price says he admires the focus displayed by Jack Nicklaus. "He's so totally focused on each shot that if you ask him, 'What do you think will happen on this hole, Jack?' he wouldn't be able to tell you because he's only thinking about the one shot that he's faced with at that moment."

"You shouldn't get mad because of a bad shot," says Curtis Strange. "For example, if you hit a bad iron shot, you still have three ways to make par. You can hit a good chip, or make a good putt, or hit a mediocre chip and a mediocre putt and still make par. If you're going to get mad, do it for making a bad score. Getting mad over a bad shot can cause you to make a bogey when your goal is to make par."

▲

Wagering

You aren't a big gambler, but because you want to be accommodating don't shy away from making wagers on the course. If the stakes get high, try making light of it or tell your playing partners that you're uncomfortable with playing for that much cash. You work hard for your money and you don't like taking big chances on losing it.

If you lose, you're gracious and praise the victors rather than complain about your poor play. If you win, you don't rub it in the others' faces.

You don't tolerate gamesmanship of any kind, nor are you willing to grant mulligans or let a partner improve a lie. Rules are rules.

▼

Payne Stewart always got irritated by partners who showed a total lack of consideration for others. "Some people are fiddling with their bags or fiddling at the tee just when you're ready to swing. Or they'll walk off the tee before you've completed your swing. Some guys will walk in front of you while you're trying to line up your putt."

▲

Let's Talk

As one of the friendliest signs in the zodiac, Aquarius can talk about virtually anything with virtually anybody.

In your contradictory nature, you enjoy being the center of attention, but you don't want people to get too personal with you. So you tend to act like a quasi emcee or television reporter, where you're in the spotlight while asking others intriguing or interesting questions about themselves. This makes some people feel important, but it can make others, like fellow Aquarians, ill at ease.

Although you'd rather not talk business on the golf course, you can hold your own against any bigwig. You'd much rather chat about the latest advances in technology for golf or computers or even about more offbeat subjects, such as feng shui or harmonic convergences.

It's important for you not to get too defensive when someone challenges your beliefs or your approach to golf. Rather than get into a debate, just laugh it off and move on to another subject.

Tee Time

You could play in 100-degree heat or 30-degree cold. Your adaptability and innovative ways dictate no special time or weather conditions in which to play that's better than another.

If you're a low-handicap player, you enjoy being matched up with partners who carry higher handicaps. You love the attention and admiration, and the others won't mind giving it—as long as you maintain an Aquarian sense of grace.

Playing Partners

Birdies

ARIES: You both are strong individuals who find each other stimulating on and off the links. You have great respect for each other and keep the personal issues to a minimum.

GEMINI: You admire each other's intellect, energy and fresh approaches to the game. You make an outstanding pairing and enjoy playing with each other because you're both so unpredictable.

LIBRA: Both of you are air signs, which helps you accept each other's different golfing styles. You each have something to offer the other: your determination and Libra's balance.

AQUARIUS: Put two Aquarians together and you never know what will happen, other than it should be a great time. During the round, you two likely will attempt shots never before tried.

Bogeys

TAURUS: Taurus is a very down-to-earth person who believes in traditional ways of playing the game. Taurus views your eccentricities as a little too far out.

LEO: To you, Leo is just too overpowering and pompous to have much fun with on the course. You don't give compliments even when Leo makes a great shot and deserves praise.

SCORPIO: Your emotional thermostats are set at opposite ends of the dial. Trying to figure each other out is about as easy as chipping in from a plugged lie.

CAPRICORN: This golfer doesn't have a clue about what makes you tick. Your swagger and innovative thinking go counter to Capricorn's disciplined, goal-oriented approach.

Pars

CANCER: You two are definite opposites. Although Cancer will never understand your unorthodox ways of doing things, this golfer can offer you good golfing tips if you're willing to listen.

VIRGO: Virgo is more of a cerebral, conservative golfer who often thinks like you do. However, Virgo has trouble understanding your eccentricities.

SAGITTARIUS: You can enjoy the fun-loving Sagittarius during a round of golf. Neither of you wants deep conversations—just a good time.

PISCES: As long as the conversation doesn't get personal, you two can be fine partners. But if Pisces tries some head games, you'll be biting golf balls in annoyance.

Peter Jacobsen

Tom Lehman

Wayne Levi

Jeff Maggert

Jesper Parnevik

Vijay Singh

Ian Woosnam

Bob Charles

Jim Colbert

Dale Douglass

Amy Alcott

Hollis Stacy

the**pisces**golfer

adaptable

good-natured

considerate

intuitive

noncompetitive

(February 20 – March 20)

As a Pisces, the last sign of the zodiac, you have the ability to adapt to virtually any situation in life, work, or play. You're not bothered if your tee time gets changed at the last moment, or the weather suddenly turns bad, or you're playing with strangers on a new course. You simply go with the flow. That's why so many people get along with you.

You possess a gentle, caring manner that makes you sensitive to the needs and concerns of others. You probably worry too much about your playing partners and not enough about yourself. You have a knack for tuning into others' psyches. You can sense if a person is sincere or not.

You go out of the way to make others feel at ease. You're always complimenting your playing partners when they make a good shot. If you can crack a self-deprecating joke, you'll do it. Part of the reason is you're really a nice person; part of it is to keep you relaxed.

▼

Battling for the lead in the 1998 PGA Championship, Steve Stricker admitted, "I was fighting my swing and fighting some [negative] thoughts." Yet he battled hard, shot 70, and finished second, two strokes behind winner and fellow Pisces Vijay Singh.

Stricker did it with a gentleman's grace so natural that it very nearly went unnoticed. He shared a joke with Singh after they both knocked in birdies on the 15th and complimented his playing partner on a perfect drive.

Because you're the kindest of all the signs in the zodiac, you tend to avoid confrontation whenever possible. As a result, you're not the most competitive person on the course. You'll lower your expectations so you won't be disappointed with the outcome if you play badly. You're a master at excuses when you don't do your best. Usually you take an I-don't-care attitude: "Golf is just a game. It's not important if I don't do well." You say it, even though you don't believe it. The top Pisces golfers had to learn that they really were better than they thought they were. You need to learn that too.

Confesses 1996 British Open champion Tom Lehman: "There were times in the past when I really wondered, 'What am I doing here?' But those are getting fewer and farther between."

In defeat, some golfers cry and some golfers laugh. Pisces tends to laugh. That's one of the reasons why you're such an endearing soul.

▼

Lehman chooses to laugh. It's the only way to deal with golf's ultimate heartbreak—losing a major in the final round. In each of the U.S. Opens from 1995 to 1997, Lehman led after 54 holes only to finish third twice and tied for second once. In the 1997 Open, he hit a seven-iron on the 17th that one-hopped into the water. Afterward, the disappointed golfer didn't get angry. Instead, mixing humility with dignity, he joked, "I would give anything in the world for a mulligan."

▲

You have a habit of seeking advice on different issues. Golf is no different. You'll ask the club pro, your playing partners, and golfers in the parking lot. The thing is, you usually know the answer; you know exactly what to do.

▼

Lehman, the third-round leader at the 1996 British Open, asked golf legend Jack Nicklaus for some advice on the eve of the final round. Nicklaus replied, "What do you need advice for? You have the game. You're solid."

When a *Golf World* reporter asked the wife of Vijay Singh, winner of the 1998 PGA Championship, who her husband turns to for swing advice, she replied, "He uses . . . everyone. If you were standing there, he'd ask you too."

▲

Equipment

You could be ambivalent about the clubs you choose. You might take this position: "I'm never going to be a good golfer, so why bother buying better clubs?" Perhaps that's true. But you should consider this position as well: "I might really enjoy the game and play better too if I bought a good set of clubs."

Try out several different models. Because you're such a sensitive, intuitive person, pay close attention to the feel of the clubs. If you're just starting out, find a set of good used clubs that give you a comfortable feeling.

Unless you're really passionate about the game, you don't need to get custom clubs.

As for accessories, just get the basics and stay away from anything flashy or expensive. They're not you, Pisces.

Attire

On or off the golf course, you feel your best when you're dressed for comfort. That doesn't mean you have no style. Quite the opposite is true. It's just that the clothes you wear should be functional and comfortable. As for style, you're suited for the classic look: a simple collared shirt and khaki slacks or shorts. Your best colors for playing are sea green and aqua.

Stay away from tight-fitting golfwear. You need room to operate, so perhaps buy either baggy fits or one size larger than what you normally wear. Cotton and other natural fabrics are best for you.

Don't skimp on golf shoes. Many Pisceans have foot problems, so a well-made comfortable shoe is absolutely important. If you neglect this area, you won't enjoy your game.

Game Preparation

One of your biggest problems is that you procrastinate. You know you should practice if you want to play well, but too often you blow it off. In fact, if you're a typical Pisces, you rarely arrive at the course early enough to go through a complete and necessary pregame routine.

Part of the reason is your resistance to being competitive. You can play well if you put your mind to it, but on the surface it appears as though you don't care to beat your friends; all you want is to have a good time on the course. However, if you examine the true nature of your feelings, you'll see that you really don't like to lose in competitive situations because it makes you feel inadequate. As a result, you take the position that winning doesn't matter.

That's why it's important to practice, because if you do— and if you take the time to prepare—you'll outshoot your playing partners, and you'll feel good about it too. You need to remember that anything worth doing is worth doing well. Practice will do wonders for you. And you just might begin to enjoy it.

▼

Vijay Singh is addicted to practice. With few interests, he enjoys spending hours on the practice range. "I've never seen anyone work as hard as that man does," says Nick Price. "The guy has torn up more practice tees. I wonder how much earth he has moved over the years because he can hit drivers and practice balls for hours on end."

▲

Your Game

Off the Tee

You should arrive at the first tee feeling fresh and calm, which can be a problem for you because of your tendency to be late. Assuming you've corrected that situation, make sure you show up at the first tee with a game plan. Mentally picture what you want to accomplish.

To you, the first few holes are crucial because they set the tone for the entire round. The better the drives, the better the chance that you'll do well.

Your success with your opening drives will propel you for the rest of the game with a positive attitude even if subsequent shots don't always go where you aimed.

If you're a typical Pisces, you could suffer from "first-tee jitters." The human body prepares for physical activity by secreting adrenaline into the blood. This shot of adrenaline gives the golfer additional strength and energy—and often anxiety. To master this natural adrenaline jolt, concentrate on converting that energy into relaxed strength, alertness, and positive thoughts.

On the Fairway

Usually, if you blow up on a hole it's because you lost confidence in your irons and reverted to the "I-don't-care" mode. The next time that happens to you, take a moment and recall your past success on the course. Try to relive a particularly good shot. Experience in your mind what it felt like when you hit that shot. Try to internalize this feeling and get back into the same thought process.

In the Hazard

So you've landed in the water or a sand trap. It's not the end of the world. It's just one shot out of the hazard. Be as deliberate and careful as possible so that it doesn't take two or three shots to escape trouble.

Because you're very adaptable in most situations, use that trait now. Don't try to blame the clubs, the wind, or anything other than your own playing abilities. Get on with the game and laugh it off. Above all, don't get into one of your "I-don't-care" attitudes. It will adversely affect your playing partners and ruin the joy of the game.

On the Green

Putting can be the best part of your game. In fact, if your match is close, you often can pull out a victory thanks to your performance on the greens.

The pressure on those six-foot putts is your friend. It causes you to concentrate harder—something that you absolutely need to do when you want to make that putt. It is said that Pisces sees only what he or she wants to see, so visualize your ball dropping in the hole. More often than not, it will.

Course Management

You must pace yourself because you don't have an abundance of energy. You don't want to wind up on the 15th hole totally tired and burned out. Also, you tend to choke on the final holes. So take your time and stay relaxed. You must maintain a positive attitude, even after you've whacked some bad shots. Play them one at a time.

Because Jeff Maggert had the most second-place finishes (thirteen) in the 1990s, people wondered if his inability to close out tournaments was from a bad case of nerves or a lack of confidence. "Maybe I press a little bit, maybe too much, knowing I've come so close so often," he admitted. "Maybe that's why I haven't won more." He made that statement shortly after winning $1 million in the 1999 WGC-Andersen Consulting Match Play Championship.

Because ultimately you believe that things will work out, you should concentrate on that positive thought when you wind up in the rough. You know your putting is better than your drives and irons, so concentrate on those strengths rather than the weaknesses of the latter.

You also should stay focused on what you do best on the course. Forget about what your playing partners are doing. Golf isn't like tennis or chess where you must react to every move your opponent makes. You need to concentrate on yourself.

▼

At the 1996 British Open, Tom Lehman had a six-shot lead in the final round against playing partner Nick Faldo, a formidable head-to-head golfer known for his methodical play and savvy determination in closing out a tournament.

"I thought maybe it was destiny, that fate was on his side," Lehman told reporters later. "I was nervous until I thought about why I was nervous. I realized I was worried about what Nick Faldo was going to do. 'Well,' I told myself, 'I can't control what Nick Faldo does. I can only control what I am going to do.' Once I started thinking about that, I was okay." Lehman won the Claret Jug.

▲

Wagering

For you, betting on the course, or anywhere else, can be troublesome. You're a great bluffer and always looking for an easy dollar. The problem comes when others call your bluff and, before you know it, you're into stakes higher than you want to be.

Team games are best for you. You'll feel less pressure and

you'll work hard because you won't want to let your partner down. Individual betting games and pushes can cause you to become too emotional to play your best.

Unfortunately, you look for an easy way out, and if you can use a little gamesmanship to rattle the other players, you'll try it. You always come up with a justification to yourself about why you play head games. Avoid this tendency by appealing to your ethical side.

Let's Talk

As a rule, Pisces isn't interested in conducting business or discussing serious subjects on the course. You do, however, like to talk about your successes, whatever your endeavor. The hardest part of your conversation is keeping yourself from embellishing your stories to make them more amusing or interesting.

If you're trying to work on a customer, you really need to watch what you say and stick to the facts. On the whole, though, you prefer not to talk business on the course. You are a fun-loving person who plays the game for the pure entertainment, not as a method to obtain a sale.

Tee Time

Because of your adaptability, you can play most any hour of the day. There is no peak time for you.

However, you're not fond of the cold—and it shows in the way you golf. So it's best not to play on cold, blustery days.

For you, high temperatures aren't a problem. You can easily adapt to the heat and humidity.

Playing Partners

Birdies

TAURUS: Neither of you takes golf all that seriously, but you both like the routine of a weekly game. This golfer's easygoing, grounded manner appeals to you.

CANCER: You both share many of the same traits—you're both gentle, caring, and sensitive. You're always seeking advice, and Cancer loves to give it.

SCORPIO: You're both water signs and have an intuitive sense about each other. This golfer understands your sensitive nature and will be there to give you that little boost.

PISCES: If it were up to you two, probably no one would even keep score. You're both out to have fun on the fairway no matter what the weather.

Bogeys

ARIES: As nice as you are, you tend to drive Aries nuts because you lack that competitive fire and energy. Aries is just too aggressive and temperamental for you.

GEMINI: This golfer's mouth will get on your nerves sooner or later. Gemini's sarcasm and lack of understanding of sensitive people like you can make you feel uncomfortable.

LIBRA: Although you share some of the same traits, you can easily tick off Libra by asking one too many personal questions—and then you'll feel badly the rest of the day.

CAPRICORN: You two aren't compatible. In your eyes, Capricorn is too driven and too aloof. Besides, you can't tolerate this golfer's quick temper.

Pars

LEO: You two can make fine playing partners because you like to seek advice and Leo likes to give it. Leo can be your cheerleader—but if he or she gets bossy, Leo can also be a pain.

VIRGO: Although you don't have a lot in common, you two tend to get along okay. However, you can get distracted by trying to figure out Virgo's hidden feelings.

SAGITTARIUS: You both are as adaptable as can be, and your golf relationship should be good, assuming Sag's big mouth doesn't somehow offend you.

AQUARIUS: As long as the conversation doesn't get personal, you two make a good pair. But if you try some head games, Aquarius will be no fun at all.